T0097927

THE CASE FOR CHILDREN

CHILDREN

Why Parenthood Makes
Your World Better

THE CASE FOR CHILDREN

CHILDREN

*Why Parenthood Makes
Your World Better*

SIMCHA WEINSTEIN

BARRICADE
BOOKS

Published by Barricade Books Inc.
2037 Lemoine Ave.
Suite 362
Fort Lee, NJ 07024
www.barricadebooks.com

Copyright © 2012 by Simcha Weinstein
All Rights Reserved

No part of this book may be reproduced, stored in a retrieval
system, or transmitted in any form, by any means, including
mechanical, electronic, photocopying, recording, or otherwise,
without the prior written permission of the publisher, except by a
reviewer who wishes to quote brief passages in connection with a
review written for inclusion in a magazine, newspaper, or broadcast.

Library of Congress Cataloging-in-Publication Data

Weinstein, Simcha.
The case for children : why parenthood makes your world better /
Simcha Weinstein.
    p. cm.
Includes index.
ISBN: 978-1-56980-474-2
1. Parenthood. 2. Children. I. Title.
HQ755.8.W423 2012
306.874--dc23

                                                    2012025175
            ISBN: 978-1-56980-474-2

        10 9 8 7 6 5 4 3 2 1

Manufactured in the United States of America

This book is dedicated to my daughter,
Orah Bina.

Whilst boys are beautiful,
nothing beats Daddy's little girl.

CONTENTS

ACKNOWLEDGEMENTS

*T*HIS IS MY first grown-up book. After two pop culture books, I knew it was time to get serious about parenting when I picked up the wrong child from day care—it happens! The following people have made this a better book and me a better father:

Carole Stuart, a publishing legend—I wish all self-described atheists were as committed to their rabbis as you are to me. Carole is a tenacious woman of high intellect who excels in humanity and humility.

My editor, Kathy Shaidle—you once told me that if all I wanted was to see my name in print, I should buy a phone book. Finally we are on the same page (pun intended). Kathy is a courageous commentator who fights for truth, justice, and the Canadian way, one blog at a time, without being muzzled by the tyranny of nice.

Dr. Allan Carlson, Phillip Longman, Kay S. Hymowitz, and W. Bradford Wilcox, scholars and brilliant authors who have all dedicated their considerable skill toward the concepts discussed in this book, giving me vital context for the formulation of my ideas—I'm supremely grateful. Please don't sue me!

Steven Bergson, Mitch Garbow, Ed Weintrob, Joshua H. Stulman, Sharon Goldinger, and Suzanne Henry—I'm grateful for your brutal critique and valuable editorial suggestions.

Rabbis Shlomie Chein, Shlomo Gestetner, Aaron L. Raskin, Yitz Creeger, and Shimon Apisdorf—thank you for your inspiration and influence.

To Rachel Fellig, the best baby photographer in Brooklyn—
thanks for taking the pictures of my children that adorn each
chapter—and making them look "normal." By the way: if any
Hollywood casting agents are interested, they are available
every day except Saturday!

George and Pamela Rohr—your infallible commitment to
Jewish causes never ceases to amaze and astonish.

The fine folks at Congregation B'nai Avraham, Brooklyn
Heights—it's always good to be connected to a synagogue
full of lawyers.

The many students, supporters, and congregants at the
Rohr Jewish Center in Clinton Hill, Brooklyn, especially the
students at Pratt Institute—you teach me the value of youth,
passion, and fashion. Fifty million slices of gefilte fish can't
be wrong!

The incredible team at the Office of Student Involvement
at Pratt Institute—Emma Legge, Meredith Crain, Alex Ull-
man, Karen Smith, and Vice President Dr. Helen Matusow-
Ayres—(black) hats off to you for supporting every single
meshugah idea I have thrown at you.

My many friends, family members, and the Manchester
City Football Club on the other side of the pond in Manchester, England—you continue to be there for me even though I
have an ever-growing beard.

My brother David and his wife, Naomi, parents, parents-
in-law, and Nanny—thank you for offering me constant love
and support.

My long-suffering wife, Ariella—you have yet to read a
single word of my previous books, so I hold out little hope

of your ever reading this. Ariella, you should know that all the wisdom contained in this book I garnered from you; just the jokes are all mine. Having opened up our home to offer hospitality to thousands of visitors at our large Friday night Sabbath dinners, which in recent years has grown to its own community center, Ariella is always happy to have me hog the limelight while she is busy making it happen.

My dear children, Mendel, Eli, Orah Bina, and Yaacov— I'm sorry that Daddy couldn't spend much time with you because he was busy writing a book about the importance of spending time with kids!

Finally, the Lubavitcher Rebbe, Rabbi Menachem Schneerson, of blessed memory—he inspired generations of young Jewish men and women to become spiritual leaders.

INTRODUCTION

The way I live my life, I wouldn't have the patience. I'd sort of want people born at the age of 10.
— Simon Cowell on fatherhood

I LIVE AND WORK in the heart of New York City, but—believe it or not—I occasionally catch a glimpse of an endangered species. I'm referring, of course, to young married couples. Even if they come to the synagogue only on the High Holidays, I'm still thrilled to meet them.

And then I say something that pretty much guarantees I won't see these couples again for another year: "So . . . isn't it time?"

The wife blushes. The husband cringes. One of them blurts out a well-rehearsed response: "Rabbi, we'd love to have kids—someday. But right now we're not ready."

That scenario plays itself out all over the world every day. An entire generation of Jewish grandmothers-in-waiting is praying impatiently for a little bundle of joy (or two or three) to spoil and fuss over.

But their daughters and sons aren't cooperating. And this isn't just a Jewish problem. Throughout the Western world, young men and women are doing everything in their prime reproductive years except reproducing. Never before in human history have birth rates intentionally fallen so far, so fast and in so many places.

I wrote this book to try to reverse this decline by inspiring young people to accept the challenge of becoming parents—and ultimately reap all the rewards that come with the awesome responsibility.

This book is intended to be a candid, honest exploration of why young people aren't having children. I work with young people every day, so believe me, I'm familiar with the arguments against parenthood. I even empathize with these people. However, I will also address all these arguments directly and demonstrate why they are flawed.

To put it bluntly, I'm advocating that couples have kids—lots of them—and have them when they are young. Quite simply, we are having children later, and having fewer of them when we do.

I realize this goes against much of today's conventional wisdom. In 2010, *Time* magazine ran a cover story by Lauren Sandler, touting the superiority of the only child.[1] Sandler explains that given the high cost of supposed "necessities" such as ballet classes and piano lessons, having more than one child these days is financially prohibitive.

However, as a father of four, I'd counter that children would rather have a brother or sister than piano lessons. (I'll have more about kids and musical instruments later.)

Jessica Valenti's 2012 hit book *Why Have Kids? A New Mom Explores the Truth About Parenting and Happiness* asks why today's smart women would be dumb enough to choose to have kids at all. Valenti cites a lot of studies in support of her thesis, yet her case is weakened by the fact that she's a mother herself!

This book is divided into three parts that I call "trimesters." In part 1, our first trimester, we'll look at why young people are putting off having children (sometimes until it is too late) or deciding not to have children at all. I also look at the population decline that's happening all over the world. The reasons are complex, and it doesn't help that so many young women have been assured that "they can always have children later." Biologically speaking, that simply isn't true. For those who've postponed parenthood until they're "ready," so often, "ready" never comes. If couples finally decide to start a family, it comes at a high price: financially, physically and emotionally. To cite just one expense: fertility treatments are often a necessity for older would be parents, but few of them realize how expensive and invasive they are.

These days, parenthood is no longer held up as a noble ideal. Fathers are scolded for bringing new little consumers and polluters into the world, and mothers in particular get grief for choosing childbearing over careers.

The parents we see in the media are often terrible role models, be they flesh and blood (the "Octomom" and Charlie Sheen) or fiction (the incompetent fathers and neurotic mothers of so many movies, television shows, and commercials).

Celebrities who dare to treat parenthood as serious business are berated. Take actress Natalie Portman. During her 2011 Oscar acceptance speech, the noticeably pregnant Portman thanked her fiancé for giving her the "most important role" of her life—motherhood. The response from some women was caustic. "Is reproduction automatically the greatest thing Natalie Portman will do with her life?" asked an agitated Mary Elizabeth Williams at Salon.com.[2] Then soccer superstar David Beckham and his wife (and former Spice Girl), Victoria, were roundly denounced for not only having a fourth child but musing in public about having a fifth. [3]

Perhaps those critics feel affronted by happy husbands like Beckham, since many of today's men seem to be taking longer to embrace adult responsibilities, including fatherhood. Books like Kay Hymowitz's *Manning Up* have sparked heated debates on the subject of masculinity. Michael Kimmel's nonfiction book *Guyland* finds, not surprisingly, that young men today "just wanna have fun." After spending their college years in a haze of alcohol and hookups, young men go on to "re-create their collegiate lifestyle in the big city," where they flock to the sort of bars that advertise "Spring Break 52 Weeks a Year."[4]

In part 2, this book's second trimester, I'll address the three most common arguments I hear against having children, which are centered on money, happiness, and the environment. I'll explain how having more children can actually be a boon to your bottom line without necessarily increasing your carbon footprint. I'll also discuss the true meaning of happiness, which society seems to have forgotten.

Part 3, the book's third trimester, covers the more transcendent reasons that parenthood makes sense. I'm a rabbi, so yes, this is the "spiritual" part, and I imagine other faith leaders will agree with my ideas. What legacy will you leave behind? I'll also speak directly to the many men and women who want children but can not have them; believe it or not, even the childless can learn from children.

Writing this book has challenged me to think more deeply about my own beliefs and actions. In the end, I made some personal discoveries that even surprised me.

As the chair of the Religious Affairs Committee at Pratt Institute, the renowned New York art school, I'm constantly awed by the talented students I interact with each day. They are tirelessly honing their skills as great designers, illustrators, and architects. In fact, our new community center was designed entirely by these students.

They do things I could never do. Their paintings and other creations are amazing. All of them are "culture vultures" who will shape the twenty-first century. Yet, while this school boasts a world-class faculty, fully equipped to impart knowledge—which is, of course, what college is for—the one thing these students don't always learn is wisdom. *Knowledge* refers to information, facts, and data. *Wisdom*, on the other hand, is the precious insight and confidence that allows us to make sensible decisions.

I'm a rabbi, not a professor. It's my job to try to impart that much-needed wisdom, even when it is unfashionable or politically incorrect. I am able to draw on my faith and thousands of years of religious tradition when confronting any topic. So, at the end of each chapter, I'll pass along a particular Jewish teaching that has given me strength and insight.

Recently, my wife and I welcomed our fourth child. The size of our family is now almost double the official national average. That fact is sure to distress many people, like those who criticized the Beckhams and Natalie Portman, those who have proudly declared themselves "childfree." I doubt many of my fellow New Yorkers would take too kindly to a male rabbi like me apparently trying to tell women what to do with their wombs. I understand that. But I can only call it the way I see it.

I'm forced to confront opposition to my family's very existence almost every day. Progressive Brooklynites don't hesitate to inform me that I'm being selfish for having so many children.

The "selfish" meme is an old one. "I would make a terrible mother," actress Katharine Hepburn liked to tell reporters. "I'm basically too selfish."[5]

We're accustomed to hearing such sentiments expressed today. However, back in the 1940s when Hepburn was a superstar, they were revolutionary—and to many ears, revolting. Men and women who dared to declare they were childless by choice were commonly denounced with a single word: *selfish*. In her own way, Hepburn embraced the word, preempting that criticism and making it almost a point of pride.

Since then, the word, and the world, has turned upside down. In the twenty-first century, we're far more likely to hear those who *do* have children described as selfish, especially if they have "too many."

Like me.

Katharine Hepburn was considered radical in her time, but that was seven decades ago, and nothing is as stale and old-fashioned as yesterday's fad. In the twenty-first century, parents have become the new counterculture. Having children makes me one of today's radicals. My hope is that this book will encourage you to become one, too.

PART 1

The First Trimester:

Why Aren't People Having Children?

Chapter 1

TOO COOL FOR KIDS?
Why People Are Putting Off Parenthood

*I'm trying to decide whether or not to have children. My time
is running out. I know I want to have children while my
parents are still young enough to take care of them.*

—Rita Rudner

*F*OR MOST COUPLES — like the ones I so bluntly confront at
the synagogue every High Holiday — the question very often
is not *if* but *when* to have children. Studies show that most
married couples who say they want to have children will have
them — eventually.

The trouble is that the longer couples procrastinate, the
more the likelihood of infertility or some other impediment

increases. In the Western world today, "ready" takes longer and longer to arrive—or never arrives at all.

This is a relatively recent phenomenon. Fifty years ago, nearly 75 percent of couples had children within the first three years of marriage. In 2010, only about 25 percent did.[1]

What changed?

That seems like a silly question. Anyone who's listened to his or her parents and grandparents talk about "the old days"—or who has watched a black-and-white movie or even a few episodes of *Mad Men*—knows that the latter half of the twentieth century was a time of great societal upheaval. The entire concept of "family" was re-examined, and in some cases, discarded. Traditional gender roles and divisions of labor were radically redefined.

What Changed for the Mothers?

Working-class women, by definition, have always worked. A small number of determined (usually privileged) women have lived untraditional lives, often as artists or scholars but occasionally as entrepreneurs or even scientists. In the mid-1940s, socialite, budding photographer, and future First Lady Jacqueline Bouvier could list her ambition in her finishing-school yearbook as "never to be a housewife" without being scolded or mocked.

However, it's possible that she was simply attuned to the burgeoning spirit of her age. In the middle of the twentieth century, one epochal event altered the average middle-class woman's traditional trajectory from child and student to married, stay-at-home mother.

With millions of men stationed overseas during World War II, American women were required to work in munitions factories and take on other nontraditional jobs. When the war ended, so did their brief experience as independent wage earners. Most of those American women married, gave birth to all those baby boomers, and generally returned to their previous homemaker roles.

Some of these women though encouraged their daughters to pursue the independence, autonomy, and adventure they had ever so briefly experienced themselves. Coincidentally, in this newly prosperous postwar America, ordinary families could finally afford to send male *and* female children to college for the first time.

Many co-eds considered college nothing more than a place to hunt for a suitable husband and graduate with what used to be called a MRS degree — that is, a marriage license to go with their diploma. Others were inspired by bestselling books such as Betty Friedan's *The Feminine Mystique*, Helen Gurley Brown's *Sex and the Single Girl*, and Simone de Beauvoir's *The Second Sex* to start questioning their lot in life.

The single career girl became a cinema and television staple. Art imitated life; not a few little girls grew up to be police officers, broadcasters, lawyers, and even astronauts because they'd been inspired by fictional heroines like Pepper Anderson on *Police Woman* and Uhura on *Star Trek*. Oprah Winfrey credits her billion-dollar television empire to the example set by Mary Richards, the fictional heroine of *The Mary Tyler Moore Show*.

The jobs these women had usually required years of expensive education and training. Feeling forced by ubiquitous feminist pop-culture messages to choose between an "exciting and rewarding" career and "boring, unfulfilling" married motherhood (and "liberated" from childbirth by the pill in the late 1960s), millions of women opted for the former. It's a pattern that's remained in place ever since.

With increased economic opportunities, even during economic downturns women no longer have a financial need to marry. In fact, the "opportunity cost" of motherhood (due to the income foregone when a woman decides to have children) has risen dramatically. Today, 55 percent of college graduates aged twenty-five to twenty-nine are female. In 2010, women earned 60 percent of all master's degrees.[2]

The twenty-first century is increasingly a woman's world. Male prospects are clearly on the wane. In 1980, women held just 26 percent of managerial positions; by 2010, that number had jumped to 51.4 percent. Women are key players in the new economic world of media, public relations, retail, design, health, and the law.[3]

Just like their male counterparts, women graduates have to pay off tens of thousands of dollars in student debt. In fact, the percentage of college grads (male and female) citing educational debt as the reason for delaying having children nearly doubled between 1991 and 2002. Ask the young people recently "occupying" cities around the world, what's a degree worth if one is required for even the most basic job?[4]

Having finally completed their lengthy and intense formal education and entered their chosen fields, many women say they end up stressed out, disillusioned, and unfulfilled. "The more women have achieved, the more they seem aggrieved," noted influential *New York Times* columnist Maureen Dowd, who claims to speak for the feminist baby-boomer generation. "Did the feminist revolution end up benefiting men more than women?"[5]

The Ticking Clock

Not incidentally, those college years happen to coincide with the prime female fertility years. Fertility begins to decline at age twenty-seven and plummets at forty. No wonder almost half of women (43 percent) with graduate degrees are childless, whether they wanted to be or not.[6] As my wife can attest, institutions of higher learning don't make life easy for students with children. Perhaps the last vestige of discrimination on campus is bias against parents.

We've set up society in such a way that men and women in their prime reproductive years are postponing having children or deciding not to have them at all. But the ideal time to have children is when you are young. Waiting has consequences. The older you get, the more set in your ways you become. At that point, making room for children seems almost impossible. You don't want to give up your favorite little self-indulgent routines and spontaneous splurges.

Not only that, but a twenty- or thirty-year-old has reservoirs of physical and mental energy a forty-year-old mother or fifty-year-old dad can only dream of. Children are work. If you've reached the age when you're having trouble partying like you used to, just imagine chasing a couple of toddlers around after working all day.

In a 2011 issue of the *New Yorker*, actress Tina Fey wrote

about her mixed feelings about having a second child: "When my daughter says, 'I wish I had a baby sister,' I am stricken with guilt and panic."[7]

She continues: "What is the rudest question you can ask a woman? 'How old are you?' 'What do you weigh?' No, the worst question is: 'How do you juggle it all?' The second-worst question is: 'Are you going to have more kids?' Science shows that fertility and movie offers drop off steeply for women after forty."[8]

Like many career women whose childbearing years are nearing an end, Fey is facing a dilemma that feminism neglected to mention: biology trumps ideology as far as fertility is concerned.

We are now so accustomed to seeing middle-aged movie stars with toddlers in tow, the average woman thinks she can put off childbearing indefinitely. Few realize how expensive, uncomfortable, and unreliable in-vitro fertilization is.

Women who have delayed pregnancy until they cannot easily conceive are now turning to having children using sperm donors (anonymous or otherwise) to try to beat the biological clock. It's a trend that's been explored in recent movie comedies such as *The Switch* with Jennifer Aniston and *The Back-Up Plan* starring Jennifer Lopez. For too many women, however, the "backup plan" is becoming their only plan, and the real-life results are often unsuccessful or financially crippling, or both.

Yet, no matter how vaguely dissatisfied some of these women may be with their lot in life, to them the idea of doing what seemed obvious to their mothers and grandmothers—getting married and having children before the age of thirty—is distasteful, impossible, or both.

In fairness to all those millions of single women across America, there's one reason that the closest many of them get to a wedding is watching (alone or with other single girlfriends) a fictional one on the big screen in the latest romantic comedy or tear-jerking drama. That reason is their male counterparts.

Where Are the Fathers?

In a November 2011 *Atlantic* cover story, Kate Bolick ponders, "As women have climbed ever higher, men have been falling behind. We've arrived at the top of the staircase, finally ready to start our lives, only to discover a cavernous room at the tail end of a party, most of the men gone already, some having never shown up—and those who remain are leering by the cheese table, or are, you know, the ones you don't want to go out with."[9]

There was a time when most men in their mid twenties had graduated from college and were well on their way to establishing their families and their careers. Today, however, visitors from another planet might be forgiven for concluding that young human males are born with both hands permanently attached to a small plastic device hooked up to a computer.

While it's true that more women than ever are playing video and computer games, the statistics are still pretty staggering: in a 2003 survey, American males aged eighteen to thirty-four reported spending thirty billion hours a year playing games—a number that has only increased exponentially in the intervening years. In fact, the average gamer's age has crept up to thirty-four. Notice that in the eight-year-old survey, that age was considered to be the upper limit for intense game playing.

Now it's the norm. An entire generation of men seems to have been regressing due to weapons of mass distraction.[10]

No wonder dating is so difficult for many women I know. Young women who've been taught since they were toddlers that they could be anything they wanted, who were encouraged to excel in sports and academics, and who were sternly instructed never to settle for second best are understandably turned off by chronically underachieving beta males. One female surgeon, for example, tells potential dates that she's a nurse so she won't intimidate them. An engineering student told me that one date bluntly informed her he would never fly on a plane engineered by a woman — to which she responded that he probably already had.

On the other hand, what incentive is there for young men to marry? Marriage is no longer a prerequisite for sex, and millions of young men have seen their fathers lose everything after nasty divorces.

What's the result? The median age for marriage in 1960 in the United States was twenty-three for men and twenty for women. Today it is twenty-nine and twenty-seven, respectively.[11]

The exceptions are young men who join the military and get to fight real enemies with tens of millions of dollars' worth of real weapons, not plastic or virtual ones. Members of the US armed services are more likely to be married and have children than their civilian counterparts.[12]

Men's Work

While the definition of what constitutes "women's work" has changed (and has been studied ad nauseam), we pay less attention to the changing roles of men in the workplace. The blue-collar worker who literally built America is an endangered species, as factory jobs migrate overseas and plants shut down. The movie *The Full Monty* offered a comical look at this trend, and while most men haven't yet been forced to become strippers to pay the bills, the metaphor is apt. How many men feel that their traditional identities have been stripped away?

In cultural terms, World War II proved to be a catalyst for men as well as women. Back from a war in which they'd endured unspeakable horrors—and enjoyed, if that's the right word, freedom from the quotidian responsibilities of marriage—a small but highly visible number of men embraced irresponsible outlaw heroes. The Hell's Angels started out as a gang of disillusioned veterans. The prosperous 1950s made it easy for hipsters to drop out of society, for Hugh Hefner to get funding to start publishing, and for the Rat Pack to embody permanent glamorous bachelorhood. It's no coincidence that the characters in the quintessential Rat Pack movie, *Ocean's 11*, all served together in the eighty-second Airborne and are cynical and bitter about their "heroism."

However, the Rat Pack was just that: a "pack" of ten men at the most, millionaires who could afford their carefree lifestyle. It was just a fantasy, and the rest of the world, watching from afar with envy or disgust, seemed to understand that. "It's Sinatra's world," went the would-be hipster's line. "We just live in it."

Today, however, nonstop hedonism is often the rule rather than the exception. So while his girlfriend (assuming he has one) dresses in business suits, today's young (and not so young) man prefers flip-flops and sweats. When she is finally ready to marry and have children, he's still too busy reading gadget magazines and playing Guitar Hero in his boxer shorts while smoking a bong. These young men and women grew up on a steady diet of *The Simpsons*. It's interesting to note that the boys grew up to be so much like irresponsible Bart and the girls so much like studious, serious Lisa.

Words of Wisdom

Let me conclude this chapter with a powerful biblical story that illustrates my point.

When the children of Israel were ready to enter the Promised Land, the tribe leaders of Reuven and Gad had been blessed with such an abundance of flocks and herds that they anticipated not having enough grazing land in Israel. So they proposed that instead of taking a portion of land within Israel proper, they would build their settlement on the Eastern side of the Jordan River, where there was more grazing land.

Moses was upset with this suggestion because, when making their request, Reuven and Gad blatantly disregarded the needs of their children and mentioned their cattle only. [13]

The leaders of Reuven and Gad then returned to Moses with a revised offer. This time they mentioned their children — but only after first speaking of their cattle. Moses again was not happy with their priorities. They were still putting business ahead of family.

Finally, they seemed to get the idea and put everything in the proper order: family first, business second.

The tribes of Reuven and Gad were making a well-intentioned mistake, one that so many of us make, too. They thought it wise to first secure a stable livelihood. Then, they reasoned, they'd be even better positioned to provide for their children.

The reason birthrates are dropping today is because so many young men and women are using the faulty equation Moses warned against: "cattle" first, children later. Some of these young people have devoted their lives to noble and important ventures. Others are "investing" in mastering World of Warcraft or acquiring a collection of shoes. However, none of these things—including money, professional status, and college degrees—are the purpose of living.

If these are our goals, then "ready" never comes. As we'll see in the next chapter, declining birthrates are happening all over the world. The consequences are dire.

Chapter 2

FROM POPULATION BOOM TO BUST:
How Shrinking Families Are Destroying Our Planet

You can't have a country where everybody lives in a nursing home.
—Carl Haub, Population Reference Bureau

$\mathcal{M}$ILLIONS OF PEOPLE are busily going about their lives—shopping, working, and watching television—blissfully unaware that the equivalent of a giant asteroid is heading toward Earth, one that seems too far away to matter until it's too late. That asteroid is the "population bust."

If you're anything like me, you're more used to hearing about the population *boom*—or, as Paul Ehrlich called it in his best-selling, hugely influential 1968 book, *The Population Bomb.*

"At the current growth rate," Ehrlich predicted at the time, "in a few thousand years everything in the visible universe would be converted into people."[1] We were assured by Ehrlich and other experts that Planet Earth couldn't handle a billion more people. We faced looming famine, drought, overcrowded cities, increases in violent crime and — ultimately — nuclear war. All these doomsday scenarios strongly influenced government policy, popular culture, and the life choices of countless individuals.

As the twenty-first century dawned, it became obvious that prediction after doomsday prediction still hadn't come true. Social scientists have recently been reevaluating all that conventional wisdom. They crunched the numbers and came to a startling conclusion.

To put it bluntly, instead of a population bomb, we're now facing a baby shortage. The number of children under the age of five is already falling in most developed nations. The United Nations projects that by 2025, that number will begin falling globally.[2]

A Worldwide Drop in Birthrates

Almost every developing country has experienced a sustained drop in birthrates. The United Nations Population Division notes that the number of births per woman has plummeted almost 50 percent, from 4.9 in the early 1960s to around 2.5 today.[3] In fact, close to half the world (including most of Europe, East Asia, and many Central and South

American countries) has a fertility rate below the replenishment rate, which demographers agree is 2.1 children per woman (although this rabbi wonders exactly how one has 0.1 child).[4] The average woman in a developed country births only 1.66 children. Without massive and consistent flows of immigration, this sub replacement fertility pattern will eventually lead to massive population declines.[5]

Throughout history, a 2.1 global replacement rate has remained steady except during catastrophic events like plague and world war. Today, though neither of these conditions exists, the replacement rate is still dropping. Throughout this book we'll investigate possible reasons why and how to change the trend. According to experts, sometime between 2020 and 2050, the world's already plummeting fertility rate will fall below global replacement rate.[6]

In 2008, this drastic situation received enormous attention thanks to a *New York Times Magazine* cover story—"No Babies?"—that surveyed international demography trends. Writer Russell Shorto noted that some countries had hit the "lowest-low fertility" mark; they were having so few babies that they couldn't replenish their numbers, even over multiple generations.[7]

Aren't Seven Billion People Enough?

If you've been following the news of late, you may be questioning my wisdom or sanity. After all, the world's overall population is growing. On October 31, 2011, the world witnessed the arrival of the world's seven billionth person, Danica May Camacho. The UN even flew the world's six billionth person, Lorrize Mae Guevarra (now twelve years old) to be there to wish her a mazel tov. According to the United Nations Project, the earth's population could hit ten million over the next ninety years.[8]

When we drill down, these numbers reveal a disturbing picture. Most of the people who will inhabit the planet in the next twenty years have already been born. This means that medical advances that improve longevity are what is really driving up the world's population. The so-called population boom is more like a "health boom." Global life expectancy has doubled, from age thirty in 1900 to sixty-five in the year 2000.[9]

We are aging faster than any functioning society has ever aged. It seems the "Golden Girls" will soon become the only girls. The rapid-aging phenomenon combined with the fertility implosion presents the perfect demographic storm, resulting in a shrinking working-age population and rapidly graying population.

Aren't These Good Problems?

"So what?" you may be asking, especially if you have heard nothing but those overpopulation scare stories your entire life. Won't the planet be better off with fewer people consuming precious natural resources and creating more pollution in the process? Won't an under populated world be a quieter and calmer place—a peaceful, prosperous paradise? Wouldn't it be nice to actually be able to find parking?

Initially, the answer is yes. Demographers call it a "demographic dividend." In the early stages of fertility decline, a nation experiences great prosperity. With fewer mouths to feed and an untapped reservoir of female workers, adults have more leisure time and disposable income. As fewer babies are born, more time and resources can be spent on them. Just look at the "tiger parenting" phenomenon in Asian countries, where small families are the norm.

Over time, this demographic dividend needs to be repaid. Fewer babies mean a smaller workforce at the same time the number of now-dependent elders explodes. The ratio of senior citizens to working-age populations becomes unbalanced. Nobody is left to cover the soaring costs of public pensions and health care.

China's boom will one day go bust. Raising a generation of well-educated and healthier children will certainly increase the country's productivity. Eventually, the "one-child" policy will reap what it sows. China's population of senior citizens will explode from 115 million in 2010 to 240 million in 2030.[10] With no national public pension system and only rudimentary health care, China will become a "4-2-1" society. That is, a single child will be responsible for two parents and four grandparents. Another side effect of the one-child policy, in which boys are favored over girls, is that there are around 120 boys for every 100 girls. To us, *Bride Wars* is a romantic comedy. In China, the phrase won't be funny.

Thus over time, the answer is no. These aren't good problems if your definition of peace and prosperity includes many things you might take for granted today, such as generous guaranteed cradle-to-grave benefits and government pensions, a constant stream of technological innovations, and other modern must-haves. That's because many of these "necessities" will soon become luxuries, and the standards of living we currently enjoy will drop dramatically without a steady stream of new humans to help provide them for us.

When it comes to demography, more is more. A larger workforce leads to innovation, efficiency, and expansion. If the next generation of the global workforce has not been born, we need to tap into our senior population for employees. And not all of these seniors will want to go back to work. We often hear that "fifty is the new forty" and "sixty is the new fifty," but this trend can't continue forever.

The United States may be the only developed country whose birthrate is clinging to the replacement level, due to a fertility rate higher than any other rich country's and a continued influx of immigrants. However, with the "great recession" of the twenty-first century, birthrates have started to slow down, just like the economy. America's advantages are that it always tends to buck the trend and it continues to value the role of family within society.

The situation is bleaker in Europe. Retirement at age fifty-five is not unheard of in many nations abroad, so as life expectancies grow longer, the tax base is shrinking. Not enough men and women are still working to pay the taxes that pay for the increasing costs of health care and pensions.

The welfare state taken for granted by Europeans is anything but well. It has flat-lined. Europeans must accept the new normal: a shrinking workforce can contribute only so much in taxable revenue. Greece is an example of a country that needs bailout after bailout from other European countries that are facing serious cuts of their own.

As the world tumbles into bankruptcy, an already over-stretched United States will inevitably be expected to police the world and keep the peace. Having borne the burden of Europe's defense expenditures since the end of World War II, America may now have to rescue (financially and militarily) other nations whose generous cradle-to-grave social programs are no longer financially viable.

What about our own social programs? In 2010 the US Social Security Administration began paying more to the elderly than it was taking in, a situation that mathematics dictates can't continue. Is an aging population likely to vote to increase the retirement age? It may have to.

Throughout the long, hot summer of 2011, rival US law-makers couldn't agree on how to balance the budget—one burdened by sacrosanct public programs such as Social Security and Medicare, which serve the country's aging (and non-reproducing) population. The budget was finally passed at the last minute but did nothing to bring America back from the brink of bankruptcy. In fact, it resulted in Standard & Poor's downgrading the country's AAA credit rating for the first time in history.

It's a depressing, scenario. What's causing it? Our confused notions about independence and interdependence. *Independence* is the word that sums up the zeitgeist of the last fifty years. Nations fought for it, women marched for it, artists celebrated it, musicians sang about it, and teenagers obsessed about it. But as we'll see in the next chapter, true independence is an illusion. So are some types of interdependence.

Words of Wisdom

In the Bible, God's first commandment to humankind is, "Be fruitful and multiply. Fill the world and conquer it."[11] Note that the emphasis is not just on having a family but on having a large one.

Some will insist that in big families, children receive less parental affection. However, I know families with only one child who is more neglected than children in a large family. That's because large families become a self-sustained support system. Divisions of labor kick in, and children naturally look after each other. Sometimes they even gang up and mutiny against the parents (which is cute to watch).

Some might ask why God needs to command people to do something that not only guarantees the continued survival of the human race but also comes so naturally. However, I sometimes wonder if that long ago command to be fruitful and multiply was actually meant for us modern people, thousands of years in the future—a kind of message in a (baby) bottle that would wash ashore in our postmodern, post-parenting era.

Chapter 3

FROM INDEPENDENCE TO INTERDEPENDENCE:
How Embracing Each Other Makes Us Better People

*For most of human history, across all societies, a 26-year old
has been considered an adult, and not starting out but
well into it. Not someone who remains a dependent
of his parent, but someone who might well have
parental responsibilities himself.*
—Mark Steyn

*T*HE RUGGED INDIVIDUAL has been the American ideal for
centuries. This seems odd because no one could have survived
alone in this strange new country hundreds of years ago.
The Pilgrims and the Puritans prospered only because their
tightly knit communities ensured that neighbor looked out

for neighbor. It helped that so many of them were interrelated through kinship and marriage.

As America grew, ties of kinship loosened. Immigrants arrived on their own, leaving their families behind, probably never to see them again. Countless Americans traveled west to seek their fortune, also bidding farewell to their relatives for the last time. With no one from "back home" to object, reinventing oneself was easy.

The *family* was no longer the basic unit of society. It was the *individual*.

A craze for self-improvement took off and continues today. Ambitious men and women created lucrative, sometimes ludicrous, personas that people around the world now think of as quintessentially American: Buffalo Bill Cody, Annie Oakley, and P. T. Barnum for example.

In the realm of American fiction, the individual is the center of the universe, usually chafing at the bit to break free of societal convention. The hero of what is arguably the Great American Novel, Huck Finn, yearns to "light out for the territory." Yossarian of *Catch-22* hates his Air Force superiors, and Updike's Rabbit and Cheever's "swimmer" yearn to escape the boring responsibilities of suburbia. From westerns like *High Noon* to dramas like *Erin Brockovich*, we're assured that one man — or woman — can make a difference.

But is all this independence and individualism really that healthy, either for society at large or for the individual? Consider the prophet of individualism: Ayn Rand. Americans polled by the Library of Congress said her still-popular bestselling novel *Atlas Shrugged* was the most influential book in their lives, next to the Bible. Meanwhile, Rand's equally famous work *The Fountainhead* still sells more than one hundred thousand copies a year, fifty long years after its debut.

The heroes of both novels are self-made, self-centered inventors and business leaders, driven not by money or power but by the thrill of accomplishment. Convinced of their own genius, Rand's willful heroes are utterly uncompromising. They thoroughly disdain popular (and expert) opinion. Naturally, they always turn out to be right in the end.

Not surprisingly, Rand is a perennial favorite with every generation of teenagers. Adolescence is the time of life when self-absorption and a yearning to break social conventions and familial bonds are at their peak.

Followers of Rand (who call themselves "Objectivists") try to pattern their lives after the lives of her fictional heroes, lauding selfishness over altruism. It doesn't occur to them that those soaring skyscrapers designed by *The Fountainhead*'s Howard Roark didn't magically build themselves or that the titans of industry lionized in *Atlas Shrugged* made their millions because lowly, ordinary peons purchased their wares and bought stock in their firms.

Tellingly, Rand's heroes are all childless, as she was herself.

The Illusion of Independence

Placing such a high value on independence makes it harder for us to accept interdependency. Embracing interdependency is essential to leading a sane, contented life.

It's no coincidence that all those rugged individuals we tend to admire are the products of make-believe. In reality, no one can survive entirely alone. We may not live in pioneer times anymore, but aren't even the most flamboyant rebels among us reliant on countless faceless folks to bring us the gas to fill up our Harleys—or to build those bikes in the first place?

Upon cursory examination, our independence is a seductive illusion. We depend on each other. Attachment to people—interdependence—is healthy and right. However, too often we shift our attachment from other people to *things* like food, homes, cars, gadgets, and trinkets. That kind of attachment is unhealthy. For example, some Harry Potter fans were so distraught when the imaginary adventure drew to a close that they went into therapy for depression! The characters in the world of Harry Potter had become their virtual family, creating a fake interdependency. When the ten-year-long fantasy finally ended, these fans were shattered.

Our detachment from others and our cultivation of virtual families is exemplified by the rise of *friend* as a verb instead of a noun in the era of Facebook.

If Facebook were a country, it would be the third largest on the planet.[1] In fact, given the real-world population declines we've been looking at, it may soon become the biggest.

Facebook's twenty-eight-year-old founder, Mark Zuckerberg—*Time* magazine's 2010 Person of the Year and one of the most important individuals on the planet—wears hoodies and sandals, looking like a grad-school student. Whereas *Wall Street*'s middle-aged Gordon Gekko—with his custom pinstripe suits and suspenders—personified the 1980s wheeler dealer, Zuckerberg is the very model of a twenty-first-century mogul.

Don't get me wrong. I'm in awe of Zuckerberg and how his creation has helped bring the world together and has transformed philanthropy and communications. For example, my parents back in England can now see their grandchildren (and give me a cross-Atlantic guilt trip) in real time. *The Social Network* (a movie that supposedly depicts the invention of Facebook with heavy helpings of irony and symbolism), though mostly fictional, nevertheless clearly had an impact on viewers and critics who made the film an award-winning box-office smash. In the film's "Rosebud" conclusion, Zuckerberg sits alone in a sterile conference room, frantically hitting "refresh" to see if the girl who once dumped him has "friended" him on his own creation now that he's become a success. Like the eponymous hero of *Citizen Kane*, Zuckerberg is portrayed as a mogul with a bottomless emotional void. Despite all his accomplishments, he supposedly remains unfulfilled. I found the conclusion chilling and wondered how many moviegoers saw their own real lives reflected in this fictional glimpse into Zuckerberg's.

According to one study, the typical user of social networking sites has around 55 real-life friends but about 121 virtual ones.[2] Just think: that's over twice as many virtual ones, and this gap is growing.

I myself have over 4,000 social networking friends, but they all happen to be real friends, too. But believe me, the low level interdependency they create in my life doesn't come close to the bond I have with my children.

That's because social networking is shallow. It creates the dangerous illusion of interdependency but one without either the risk of intimacy or the burden of responsibility. No doubt this is part of its appeal to the perpetual adolescent. However, no truly successful life can be based upon an illusion.

It's revealing that one of the most popular movies of the twenty-first century so far is *Avatar*, in which the hero chooses his second, virtual life over his first. Around the world, *Avatar* fans chat online (of course), teach themselves Na'vi (the film's fictional language), and paint themselves blue, trying to manufacture a virtual reality in the real world. We may laugh at such people, or pity them, but we might also ask ourselves, "Do I do more or less the same thing, without the costumes and lingo? Don't I inhabit a virtual world that seems like a community, but that really revolves around me?"

Alone Together

I'm surrounded by young people all day. As I look around, I see a generation tapping away at their personal laptops and smart phones while they wait for their daily coffee fix. In 1989, there were 585 coffeehouses in the United States; now there are over 24,000.[3] Walking into Starbucks feels like entering an adult nursery. (Have you noticed that society has gone from *Cheers*, where "everybody knows your name" to Starbucks, where the employees have to write your name on your latte so they'll remember to shout it out?)

Sometimes young people send each other texts or e-mails from one chair to another—only a few feet apart. Believe me, I know: I must confess that I asked my wife to marry me via e-mail when we were sitting in an Internet café in Jerusalem, both tapping away on separate computers. At the time, I was trying to be ironic by choosing such an informal method of communication to pop such a serious question.

We are essentially "alone together," to borrow the title of MIT Professor Sherry Turkle's controversial 2011 book. Turkle observes: "If you get into these e-mail, Facebook thumbs-up/thumbs-down settings, a paradoxical thing happens: even though you're alone, you get into this situation where you're continually looking for your next message, and to have a sense of approval and validation."[4]

Great. Now we all have *two* images to obsess about: our flesh-and-blood body and face and the avatar we oh-so-carefully choose to represent us on Twitter. In a weird way, our avatar becomes the little "me" we send out into the world. It becomes our baby.

In our binary world, you're either a number one or a zero. But in real life, we aren't data. When my son wakes up after a bad dream, I can't console him with a 140-character tweet.

Moving Home

Unfortunately, a kind of reverse interdependency has become acceptable over the last ten years or so. That's the phenomenon of adult children moving back in with their parents.

Instead of moving out to start their lives, they are moving back home to avoid them. Some feel they have no choice.

What happened? Science fiction promised us that the twenty-first century would usher in a new era of gleaming inventions and astonishing progress. For a while, with every new must-have gadget, that promise was becoming "science fact."

However, the tech stock bubble had to burst eventually. When it did so in 2000, unemployment began to rise as more jobs were outsourced to other countries. Then the collapse of Fannie Mae and Freddy Mac in 2008 deepened an already developing worldwide recession. Blue chip companies that had been around for decades collapsed. The entire planet seemed to be going backward instead of forward, and so did the younger generation.

Recent college graduates couldn't find work or were the first laid off as the economy faltered. Unpaid internships became the only way to break into many prestigious industries and therefore became more coveted and competitive. Burdened with tens (sometimes hundreds) of thousands of dollars of debt, these twenty-somethings began moving back home with their parents—a trend that shows no signs of letting up. Social scientists call them the "boomerang generation."

You might think that, as an advocate of interdependence, I'd be delighted by this trend. I'm a big fan of President Obama's decision to move his mother-in-law into the White House, creating one big happy (three-generation) family. I truly hope his example will encourage others to abandon the modern paradigm of shuffling seniors off to nursing homes.

However, there's all the difference in the world between parents moving in with their kids and children moving back in with their parents. It's the difference between moving forward and moving backward.

In the latter instance, these children are sometimes reluctant to embrace adult responsibilities. Having been raised by "helicopter parents" who chauffeured them to play dates and scheduled their every waking moment, it's no wonder contemporary twenty-somethings are reluctant to break free. They don't know how.

Today, many young college graduates admit that moving back home no longer carries a stigma. All their friends are doing it, and it's more comfortable and convenient than dealing with landlords, leaky roofs, and utility bills. Their childhood homes likely boast well-stocked refrigerators, not to mention all those cool electronic gadgets.

Here some will point out that those graduates are lucky they don't have children already. Being unemployed and a parent has got to be a worst-case scenario, right? But I'd argue that unemployed mothers and fathers are even more motivated to find work than their childless counterparts.

Waiting to Grow Up

The women in the insanely successful *Sex and the City* television franchise obsessed about men but the cast of women didn't seem to need them because they'd assembled their own family consisting of other women just like themselves. These women had sex "just like men," casually and consequence free.

At the end of the last century, the term *hooking up* started gaining popularity to describe the no-strings-attached sexual behavior of college kids. Then we started hearing about "friends with benefits," a more serious — if that's the word — form of the same basic arrangement, except it was long term rather than a one-night stand.

Inevitably, the phrase lent its name to a 2011 romantic comedy starring Justin Timberlake and Mila Kunis. The same year saw the release of an almost identical film with Ashton Kutcher and Natalie Portman.

Being a rabbi, I generally prefer more modest fare, so I haven't seen either film. However, I'd be willing to bet (and I don't usually gamble, either) that both feature dark-haired female leads (not the dumb-blonde floozy stereotype) portraying high-powered, successful professionals who live in gigantic apartments they couldn't possibly afford in real life and who don't have time for commitment any more than the men in their lives do. Yet human beings are not wired for emotion-free relationships, a conclusion I'm sure the movies make (spoiler alert!).

More and more, women are wondering if they're better off without men. Maureen Dowd certainly seems to thinks that the opposite sex is obsolete. The *New York Times* columnist whose books include 2005's *Are Men Necessary?* After all, if so many of the "eligible" bachelors out there would rather play with an Xbox or party with their friends than go out with women, what are women supposed to do?

These young men admire man-child actors like Vince Vaughn, Owen Wilson, Jonah Hill, Seth Rogan, Jack Black, Matthew McConaughey, Jason Siegel, and Paul Rudd. In movie after hit movie, the postmodern Peter Pan is the instantly recognizable hero, and the plots illustrate the zeitgeist a little too perfectly. From *Old School* (2003), in which three grown men decide to start a college fraternity, to 2011's *The Change-Up*, in which a husband and father gets his wish to trade places with his single, free-spirited buddy.

However, sometimes a jewel pops up in the pop culture

dross. *The Graduate*—a touchstone film for disaffected youth in the 1960s—ended anticlimactically with the runaway lovers experiencing the briefest of euphorias before the magnitude of what they've done dawns on them in the backseat of the bus. In contrast, there's no such bittersweet tinge of regret in *Knocked Up*. Forced to reluctantly assume responsibility after an evening of careless, drunken passion results in pregnancy, two mismatched accidental parents (including one stereotypical slacker) experience unimagined happiness. Yes, *Knocked Up* was just a movie, but it pointed out a paradoxical truth: babies are born, but parents aren't—they're *made*.

The point is, if you wait to grow up before you have kids, you might never get around to doing either.

Words of Wisdom

"And Isaac . . . took Rebecca, and she became his wife, and he loved her."[5] Note that the Hebrew Bible says Isaac married Rebecca, built a home with her, and *then* he loved her. Of course, he loved her before he married her, but he didn't marry her because he was carried away by fleeting emotions disguised as love. For him and Rebecca—and all happily married couples—real love comes later.

From our twenty-first-century perspective, seen through the twin lenses of independence and instant gratification, this setup sounds backward. We expect to fall in love and then (maybe) get married and then (maybe) raise a family—assuming we expect to do any of that at all.

This is because we confuse love with attraction and infatuation. So many romantic comedies end when the hapless couple finally gets engaged or—maybe—celebrate their wedding. In reality, that's when the best part of the story really starts.

True love requires work. When the wedding is over, the marriage—and the real work—begins.

I could fill pages with lists of the movies, magazines, and television shows all about planning the perfect wedding. What we could really use are a few guides to planning the (im)perfect marriage.

Marriage has survived as an institution in many forms (some good, some not so good) for thousands of years because marriage works—at least for those willing to put in the work required. Married couples are better off financially, emotionally, and even physically. Studies going back *140 years* prove that married men live longer than single ones.[6]

Of course, planning your new life with children is essential, partly because it helps mentally prepare you for the daunting task ahead. However, you can't use perpetual planning to put off taking action and making tough decisions—like whether to become a parent.

Having a baby can be scary, to put it mildly. Motherhood demands a shift from a lifelong focus on oneself to a concentration almost exclusively on another. Fatherhood also demands responsibilities and commitments that society no longer demands of men or prepares them for. As many parents will tell you, children were the catalyst that finally forced them to grow up. This can be a bittersweet transition, but growing up bestows rewards of its own.

Maybe that doesn't make for a typical Hollywood ending, but that may not be a bad thing after all.

PART 2

The Second Trimester:

*Why Children Can Be Good for
Your Budget, Your Happiness,
and the Environment*

Chapter 4

MILLION-DOLLAR BABIES:
The Real Cost of Having Kids

There is nothing complicated about finance. It is based on old people lending to young people. Young people invest in homes and businesses; aging people save to acquire assets on which to retire. The new generation supports the old one, and retirement systems simply apportion rights to income between the generations. Never before in human history, though, has a new generation simply failed to appear.
—David P. Goldman

IT WAS AFTER midnight. Our kids were finally asleep. I took advantage of the rare quiet time to do my taxes online, hoping I wouldn't owe Uncle Sam too much money again this year. Living in Brooklyn is expensive, especially when you have three children.

I was working up the nerve to hit "send" on my return when my wife waved a little white plastic wand between me and the computer screen. That familiar "thin blue line" on the pregnancy test silently spoke volumes.

At that moment, was I overcome with joy? Did I think of my children's smiles when they learned they'd be getting a new baby brother or sister? No. I started to sweat.

Where are we supposed to put four children in a two-bedroom condo?" I thought. "My new car fits only three in the back. First more diapers, then medical bills, then Hebrew school fees," my mind raced.

How Expensive Are Babies, Anyway?

Kids are expensive—very expensive. Today's college graduates are entering a job market that's as grim as that in the 1930s. Money is most often cited as the reason couples choose to postpone parenthood, sometimes permanently.

What does it really cost to raise a child from birth through age seventeen? The US Department of Agriculture (don't ask me why it's the one in charge of calculating this) puts the figure at about $250,000 as of 2009. "For the overall United States," it reports, "annual child-rearing expense estimates ranged between $11,650 and $13,530 for a child in a two-child, married-couple family in the middle-income group."[1]

Phillip Longman, in his book *The Empty Cradle: How Falling Birthrates Threaten World Prosperity and What To Do About It*, points out that the department's calculations don't even include any provision for a child's college tuition. He adds that these figures also don't take into account the invisible opportunity costs of a typical middle-class couple's lifestyle choices. If the wife quits her job to stay home with her child, "her commitment to motherhood will wind up costing her $823,736 in foregone income by the time her child reaches 18."[2] Hence Longman's nickname for today's children: "million-dollar babies."

No wonder I was sweating when my wife showed me that positive pregnancy test. When presented as a seven-figure lump sum—one that doesn't include college tuition—the cost of having children makes parenthood sound impossible (unless you win the lottery).

However, when approached from another, more realistic, angle, those numbers aren't that scary. We were looking through the wrong end of the telescope. After all, we live day-to-day and year-to-year, not all at once.

Financial expert Dave Ramsey advises parents-to-be to calm down. "Believe it or not," he says, "babies aren't that expensive." An old-fashioned advocate of strict budgeting and paying down consumer debt, the parsimonious money guru admits that his kids "grew up wearing so much consignment clothing that they thought OshKosh B'gosh came from yard sales."[3]

Not surprisingly, Ramsey advises expectant couples to "stop the debt snowball" and save as much money as they can, beginning immediately. He advises putting aside money into an Education Savings Account as soon as a child is born to cover college expenses.

Parenthood forces you take your finances seriously, maybe for the first time in your life. This is never a bad thing. The fact is, I make more money now than I did before I became a father—I have to! I was obligated to become more industrious.

Parents-to-be should also draw up wills and review their life insurance to reflect their new responsibilities. In general, married parents spend more money on insurance than adults who are single and childless.

When you have children, your expenses increase, but remember: they also shift. You won't be spending as much on personal indulgences anymore and you'll be going out less. I admit that doesn't immediately sound very positive, but believe me: staying in with your baby is entertainment all its own. Besides, you'll be too tired to do much socializing, anyway.

However, remember that couples also need time together to get a break from bottles and babies. My wife and I have a weekly date night. Admittedly, it happens only about once a month, but the intention is there. On those special nights, my in-laws come over to baby-sit, and they are usually kind enough to foot the date night bill, too—another money saver!

Cheaper by the Dozen?

In real terms, having children has actually never been cheaper, and having a big family makes more sense now than ever before. Over the last ten years, the prices of baby necessities—like diapers, wipes, formula, cribs, and clothes—have actually decreased.[4]

My wife and I make our own baby food. It's fun, healthy, and much more affordable. Not to mention the miracle of mother's milk, which has saved us even more money.

The current economy can actually work to your advantage.

Real estate is practically being given away, and interest rates are at their lowest in decades (meaning that mortgage rates are lower than ever). I doubt we will ever see circumstances like these again in our lifetimes. As long as people did not pull out of the stock market during the crash and kept up their regular 401(k) payments and employee matches, they are quite likely wealthier than before the crash.

Children really are cheaper by the dozen. Economies of scale kick in. It's just a matter of throwing a little more pasta into a larger pot. The more children I have, the more I recycle (more on that important subject later). Just because we have four children doesn't mean we have four of everything. After all, we need only one changing table at a time, and my younger son doesn't know or care that he's wearing his older brother's clothes.

One of the best ways to reduce the cost of parenting is to reach out to family and friends. Your coworkers with older children will be thrilled to get those used cribs and baby clothes out of their house or garage.

Remember, too: there are tax credits and government programs designed especially to help parents that didn't exist even a decade ago. This trend is likely to continue as the population bust continues.

Joining the Children's Network

Children are a vital source of social capital. As I meet other parents at play dates and PTA meetings, my horizons are broadened. Some people fear that having children will cut them off from their childless friends and from the outside world in general. However, my experience has been exactly the opposite. Through my children, I've been introduced to a new social world that has brought my family many blessings.

The twenty-first century is all about networking, and children offer plenty of opportunities to build fruitful connections with others. To cite just one example, I've bonded with my co-workers over garbage bags of old children's clothes and toys, as we gratefully pass along resources. Having children means arranging play dates, sitting with other parents at school and sports events, and otherwise immersing yourself into a whole new world. The experience obliges you to broaden your horizons. Children can even lead to jobs and work contacts.

Much more importantly, children strengthen bonds within families. Grandchildren add a new dimension to your relationships with your own parents. Along with providing emotional support, grandparents, if they are able, are notoriously generous with their grandchildren. Some may well want to help out with their grandchildren's tuition payments or a down payment on a first home. While they might not be that keen on buying their thirty-year-old man-child an Xbox, splurging on one for the man-child's child is a different matter.

A Rare Commodity

Have you noticed how protective people are of their children these days? When I was growing up, our mothers practically kicked us out of the house in the morning and told us not to bother coming back home until the streetlights came on. Anyone over the age of forty will tell you a similar story.

And believe me, my mother wouldn't have sent us out wearing a convict-style GPS bracelet so she could track our every move. I expect that soon those bracelets will be obsolete. The same GPS technology will eventually be implantable, and helicopter parents will be clamoring to get a chip for their child. [5]

Perhaps because people are having fewer children, they're subconsciously thinking of them as a rare commodity. Obviously, children *are* precious. But when families had three or more children, mothers didn't feel obligated to chauffeur them everywhere or go to every pageant and ball game. Kindergarten "graduation"? Our parents would have scoffed at the idea. Now failure to attend such events might be considered tantamount to child abuse. Watching my kids getting their diplomas wearing caps and gowns *and* diapers did feel a little, well, childish.

When parents have only one or two children to spoil, gifts get more expensive and elaborate and even come to be regarded as necessities. Consider the rise of the Bugaboo. This "Cadillac of baby strollers" has tires fit for Formula One, not baby formula. A Bugaboo can set parents back $1,000, and many grudgingly pay that amount because they're afraid of being judged by the other parents in the neighborhood for not giving their baby the best of everything. No wonder they sigh that they can't afford kids.

Factor in the longer hours Mom and Dad work to — you guessed it — pay for the stroller, and they have less time to care for the baby themselves. So they have to hire a nanny, and that costs money, which means working longer hours — and so on.

Keep in mind that many things you think your child needs aren't really necessities. However, in today's materialistic, consumerist society, we're under more pressure than ever to keep up with other parents in terms of toys and clothing. In a hundred years, we've evolved from an agricultural economy — in which children were a family's "employees" — to a society in which kids are the boss. Even if your children don't make constant demands for gifts, you're surrounded by advertising and entertainment messages telling you you're a lousy parent if your kids don't receive all the latest goodies.

While the recent economic downturn has slightly dampened the craze to show off our "designer children," that yearning still lingers just beneath the surface for so many of us. We can't reprogram our own — or our peers' — high expectations and aspirations overnight.

Don't Try to Be a Perfect Parent

Before we spend money we don't have on a trendy baby item, we can ask ourselves, "Am I buying this for the sake of my child or am I trying to impress others and live up to an impossible standard of perfect parenting?" Visit thrift stores or try eBay to find what you want. Do you think my kids even know or care that their Ralph Lauren sweater cost $1? (And the other parents won't know, either, unless you tell them.)

Here's an example from my own life. My wife and I used to schlep our six-year-old Eli to hipster Williamsburg for violin lessons, where the (childless) teacher treated her students like prisoners of war. After two years watching the poor kid desperately try to play "I Like Chocolate Ice Cream," we were forced to admit that these classes were more about making us look and feel like super-parents than about enriching our son's life. He's happy to play at home by himself. We yanked him out of the class, saving ourselves a small fortune and saving him further embarrassment. We couldn't even tell ourselves later that our intentions had been good. We were trying to look selfless while being self-centered.

Judith Warner looked at this troubling trend in her book *Perfect Madness*. See if this sounds like your mental picture of parenthood: "I signed my un-athletic elder daughter up for soccer. Other three-year-olds in her class were taking gymnastics, too, and art, and swimming and music. I signed her up for ballet. I bought a small library of pre-K skill books."[6]

If it does, you may want to rethink your "Martha Stewart" approach to parenting. This approach is not just financially expensive; it's a fad that may be taking a toll on our children and on society at large.

As the offspring of the first wave of helicopter parents come of age, Warner is noticing that over-babying our babies has its downside: when we raise children to think they are the center of the universe, they become bitter and confused when they realize everybody else was raised to think they were too. We used to think that only neglect caused these kinds of behaviors in children. Now it seems clear that over-parenting leads to the same outcomes. Does an entire planet populated with disrespectful, spoiled, undisciplined, self-centered adults (who all hate the violin) twenty years from now sound like paradise or hell on Earth?

So don't feel guilty about not being able to give your children everything. By refusing to ride the perfect-parent rollercoaster, you may be giving them (and humanity) the greatest gift of all.

Children and the Future

In a particularly ridiculous line in the famously bad movie *Plan 9 from Outer Space,* a psychic solemnly intones, "We are all interested in the future, for that is where you and I are going to spend the rest of our lives!" Naturally, we laugh (or groan) at that blatant statement of the obvious, yet how often do we consider the consequences that our present day decisions will have, particularly when we decide not to have children?

"So what?" you may respond. "The world will be a better place with fewer people!" That's been the conventional wisdom for decades. We're told there will be fewer mouths to feed, for example, and that hospitals will be less crowded. But think about it: fewer people also means fewer people to grow and prepare the food—and fewer doctors, nurses, and pharmacists, too. If limited resources are your major concern, bear in mind that an ever-increasing elderly population will consume far more resources than children do.

As author and self-proclaimed "demography bore" Mark Steyn likes to say, "The future belongs to those who show up for it."[7] We may think that a future without as many children will be identical to the present except maybe a little quieter.

Not so. As noted in the first chapter, a sustained drop in fertility will have a far-reaching impact in terms for funding our Social Security system which was designed with the assumption that the nation's birthrate would always stay healthy. For example, when the United States instituted its Social Security program, sixteen workers were paying into the system for every retiree. Today the number of workers is three.

Aging populations present other financial problems. Fewer young workers and higher tax burdens don't make a good recipe for innovation and growth. Also, fewer people leads to declining markets—and thus to less business investment and formation.

Many people claim they can't afford to have children, but in many respects, as a society we can't afford not to. Innovation and technological breakthroughs tend to be a young person's game. Even if you aren't swayed by all the "policy wonk" talk about Social Security's shrinking tax base, consider this: technological, artistic, and cultural developments are overwhelmingly spurred on by young people, who are more willing and able to take risks.

We take progress for granted, but we shouldn't. You can't remove an important element (in this case, a new generation of children) from any equation and realistically expect to get the same end result.

Choosing Children and Making It Work

I'm not saying choosing parenthood is easy, but nothing worthwhile ever is. After our first child was born, my wife told me she wanted to go back to school. Fortunately, my work schedule is fairly flexible, so we were able to support each other and share responsibilities. At first, my wife took a night class. Then a morning class. Then a Sunday class. Then she started going to school full time.

It would be disingenuous to say that the situation was not frustrating for both of us. We would sometimes pass each other in the doorway, exchanging little more than a sigh. But as I write this, she has just finished her master's degree and is working as a special education therapist (and I have learned to be an excellent cook, if I do say so myself).

Our family's situation isn't unusual. Increasingly, companies that want to hang on to good employees are increasingly offering more child-friendly work environments. In 2012, TechCrunch.com noted that Marissa Mayer, the newly appointed CEO of Yahoo!, may be "the first ever pregnant CEO of a Fortune 500 tech company," hailing the appointment as "trailblazing." Another tech power-player, Facebook's COO Sheryl Sandberg, is also a working mother. She made news around the same time, when she said she made a point of being home for dinner with her family after work.[8]

Telecommuting is no longer considered exotic. Employers are more flexible when it comes to accommodating a parent-employee with a child. We still have a long way to go, but the trend is headed in the right direction for anyone worried about how to balance work and family.

Having four children has challenged me financially, to put it mildly. I don't have the resources to buy my children everything they want, but frankly, I think that's a good thing. I think they do, too—at least much of the time. I've noticed that they get bored with their high-end presents pretty quickly but ask me to read the same storybook to them hundreds of times.

Toys are wonderful and violin classes and yoga lessons are okay, but the truth is that kids would rather just play with kids. Invest in a brother or sister for your child instead!

How to Become a Millionaire

Let me play devil's advocate: let's agree that a baby does in fact cost you $1 million.

Congratulations: you now have an asset worth $1 million. You're a millionaire! Would I part with one of my "assets" for $1 million—or even $100 million? Not on your life! If you think of children as assets instead of liabilities, you suddenly see parenthood from a different viewpoint. Yes, in purely material terms, children are expensive. Yet they're also a priceless blessing and the best investment you can make in terms of your—and society's—future.

Words of Wisdom

The Talmud tells us about Rabbi Eliezer, an eminent sage of his day. He was once asked, "How far must one take the holy act of honoring father and mother?"[8]

Rabbi Eliezer recounted a story of a certain idol worshipper named Dama ben Natina, who possessed a precious stone that was required for the service of the high priest in the holy temple. A group of sages from Jerusalem came to see Dama ben Natina and offered him a great sum in exchange for the stone.

But Dama ben Natina turned down their offer—for a surprising reason: the key to the safe containing the jewel was under the pillow his father was sleeping on.

He asked the visitors, "Shall I sell you the honor due to one's father and mother for money?"[9]

This may seem like a quaint yarn of old, but it contains an eternal truth: the love between a child and parent is worth more than money.

Chapter 5

PARENTHOOD AND HAPPINESS:
All "Oy" and No Joy?

We spend more but have less; we buy more but enjoy less;
we have bigger houses and smaller families; more
conveniences, yet less time. We have multiplied
our possessions, but reduced our values.
—Bob Moorehead

*A*MERICA WAS FOUNDED, in part, on the ideal of "the pursuit of happiness." Two centuries later, however, the pursuit isn't enough for us. We want guaranteed happiness on demand. The exhausting daily chores and sacrifices that parenthood requires are the last thing we think will help us achieve it. After all, who wants a bunch of time-consuming, noisy, unpredictable children around, interrupting our pursuit of happiness?

The trouble may not be children per se, but our own shallow definitions of *happiness*. As a famous *New York Magazine* article dared to declare in 2010, parenting is "All Joy and No Fun."[1] Throughout the article, Jennifer Senior cites study after scientific study, "proving" that having children makes parents unhappy.

That's another thing that sets us apart from our ancestors: our insatiable appetite for scientific proof. We're convinced that everything can be studied and quantified—even happiness. In what sounds like a satirical skit, both the British prime minister and the French president are now considering adopting a "gross national happiness" measurement to take its place alongside the traditional gross domestic product.[2]

We've become so accustomed to using science and studies to prove the rightness and truth of things we want to believe, we forget that not everything in life can be measured and computed. Even that writer for *New York Magazine* starts to wonder how we define and measure something as elusive and ephemeral as happiness. "Is happiness something you *experience?*" she asks. "Or is it something you *think?*"[3]

In an epiphany of sorts, Senior notes, "for many of us, purpose *is* happiness. " She goes on: "Martin Seligman, the positive-psychology pioneer who is, famously, not a natural optimist, has always taken the view that happiness is best defined in the ancient Greek sense: leading a productive, purposeful life. And the way we take stock of that life—in the end, isn't by how much fun we had, but by what we did with it. (Seligman has seven children.)"[4]

I smiled when I saw those parentheses. To my way of thinking, the unusually large size of that expert's family isn't an amusing aside or an incidental factoid. It's one of the lengthy article's most revealing sentences but one that's practically hidden by those parentheses and offered up as an afterthought.

Martin Seligman may be a highly trained social scientist, but he's also a father. His mature, old-fashioned conclusions aren't based just on interviews with other people and number crunching. They can't help but be informed by his own life experience.

Like Seligman, I think we need to examine our definition of *happiness*. We have come to equate happiness with pleasure instead of purpose. Pleasure seekers need to constantly maximize their pleasure because the Law of Diminishing Returns kicks in and they become jaded.

We've also mistakenly come to believe that the opposite of pleasure is pain, when the actual opposite of pain is *no pain*—a dull, empty state. When we're in this state, we continually try to find a new anesthesia to comfort us and maximize our pleasure. Unfortunately, the harsh reality is, pain and struggle are unavoidable realities of life. Those who've tried to live in violation of this simple fact have always failed miserably.

Comfort may be very comforting, but it's not ultimate pleasure. Worse, it requires constant replenishment. Look at eBay. It became a billion-dollar success because so many people needed a giant dumping ground for all the garbage they thought would bring them pleasure, when all it did was bring them momentary comfort. You'll notice the Founders didn't say anything about the "pursuit of comfort."

All the studies about parenthood and happiness have it only

half right. Yes, parenthood is hard and painful and requires sacrifice. However, real pleasure is inseparable from pain. There is no greater example than childbirth itself (although as my wife would quite rightly tell you, that's easy for me to say). So I'll let her say it: "Yes, childbirth is the greatest pain I have ever experienced," she says, "but it's also the greatest pleasure."

Delaying Gratification

Allow me to try to cut through this confusion by citing just one more study: the Netflix test. If you're a Netflix member, you've got a list of movies in your queue that you think you might want to watch someday. According to the Netflix test, if you're a typical member, your queue lists lots of "good-for-you" films: award-winning documentaries and deep, serious dramas. In one experiment, though people who were told they could pick one movie to watch immediately almost always opted for a lowbrow, "junk-food" flick instead.[5]

The Netflix test is to adults what the "marshmallow test" is for kids. The marshmallow tests, carried out in the 1960s and 1970s, gave children the option of eating one marshmallow immediately or waiting a short time and being rewarded with two. Both tests demonstrate whether or not someone can practice delayed gratification.

If immediate gratification is your only goal in life, having children — and enduring the here-and-now physical pain, financial strain, and emotional turbulence — is the last thing you'll place in your queue.

However, have you ever noticed that a whole day of eating

nothing but junk food or an entire night wasted watching trashy movies leaves you feeling strangely empty, if not downright discontented? Then here's my friendly warning: going through your entire life that way will leave you feeling just as empty. Giving in to the desire for immediate gratification may well make you happy, but only a life lived thoughtfully with a transcendent purpose is ultimately satisfying.

Maybe You Have to Be There

Not even Apple has invented an app that can measure the wonder you feel when your son or daughter falls asleep on your chest while you marvel at your child's perfect little fingers and toes. Do you think that sounds corny? I used to think so until I experienced the sensation myself.

Real wisdom about the phenomenon of happiness is something you won't learn from studies and surveys. To truly understand the joy that comes from being a parent, you have to be one.

The happiness I experience being a father can't be measured. Rereading old storybooks with my children, I see the world anew with un-jaded eyes.

Of course, this isn't the same thing as trying to relive your childhood. Having written a book about superheroes, I've spoken at lots of comic book conventions, and it saddens me to see thousands of grown men and women living vicariously, playing make-believe in their elaborate costumes. Watching men my own age dressed as Jedi knights having light-saber fights in the hotel lobby is funny for a minute or two, but ultimately it's a little weird. Once again, we see people trading true happiness for temporary comfort, maturity for nostalgia, and true family for a fragile arbitrary "community."

It's Not Your Happiness versus Theirs

Many people fear that being forced to focus on their children's happiness will compromise their own. However, one of the paradoxes of parenthood is that just the opposite is true. You and your children will be happier if you don't focus on their happiness quite as much.

Think about it this way: every time you fly, the airline tells you to put on your own oxygen mask before you place one on your child. This instruction goes against every natural instinct, but you realize how wise it is if you give it a moment's thought. You won't be able to look after your child properly until you look after yourself first.

The same principle applies to our everyday lives, not just on planes during an emergency. Parents too often give up their own leisure time and try to "kill two birds with one stone" by spending all their free time in activities with their children. We think this makes us better parents, but much of the time either we're bored or the children are.

Let's face it: most activities trumpeted as "fun for the whole family" rarely are. When we use up all our free time going to child-centered events, we're bored and our children know it. On the other hand, try taking your children to more adult venues and watch them grow impatient and start acting out. The day I schlepped our children to the Museum of Modern Art was an unforgettable experience—in all the wrong ways.

I'm not advocating never taking the kids to highbrow, cultural places or leaving them in front of the television all day. (In fact, our family doesn't have a television.) But contrary to that warning sign you see in the supermarket, sometimes it's okay to leave your child unattended in the sense of not feeling obligated to schedule every moment of his or her day (and yours) with busyness for the sake of being busy. Allowing children to just "be" is the only way they will develop intellectual curiosity. Lenore Skenazy in her book *Free-Range Kids* advises just such a hands-off approach as best for parents and kids.[6]

Such advice would have seemed like common sense to previous generations of parents. But parenting has changed a lot in the last few decades. Men are spending far more time with their children than their fathers did with them. Meanwhile, many working mothers, in an attempt to make up for spending all that time at the office, are also trying too hard to turn every second into "quality time." This sounds like a positive trend, but as I've noted before, we need to ask ourselves whether we're being helicopter parents in order to meet our children's true needs or if we're under enormous massive peer pressure to be seen as perfect parents.

Much of the time, my daughter would rather watch a giant purple dinosaur named Barney than spend time with me. My children are perfectly happy to come up with their own activities. In this way, they develop their imaginations and independence—and I get some time to myself.

Words of Wisdom

The psalmist King David noted, "Those who plant with tears will harvest with joy."[7] That ancient message has withstood the test of time because it reflects the unchanging pattern we see in nature. When we plant a seed, we're making a sacrifice because the seed is planted, not eaten. We choose delayed gratification and long-term satisfaction.

The rewards for making this choice are enormous. You can confirm this if you turn to your family and friends and ask them about the most important things in their lives. They will place their children near or at the top of their list. They probably won't mention their car or their last vacation or the last party they went to.

Take me, for example. Having a birthday on New Year's Eve means I've always had a double excuse to party. Yet my most memorable December 31 was the one that fell in 2009. That night, I wasn't at a party. I was nervously waiting for the birth of my first daughter in the Maimonides Medical Center.

Shortly before midnight, I received the best birthday gift ever: a beautiful baby girl. I already had two wonderful sons, but there really is something special about "daddy's little girl." Believe me, I didn't need fireworks, champagne, or that glittering ball dropping in Times Square to celebrate that New Year's Eve.

Chapter 6

SAVING THE PLANET:
Are Babies Bad for the Environment?

*We'll be eight degrees hotter in thirty or forty years, and
basically none of the crops will grow. Most of the people
will have died, and the rest of us will be cannibals.*

—Ted Turner

$\mathcal{W}$HILE MY WIFE was pregnant with our fourth child, she
was called for jury duty. Since her due date was looming, her
doctor wrote a letter to the court, asking for an exemption.
When I went to the courthouse office to deliver the letter (my
wife was at work), I was taken aback by how long the line
was. Everyone had a reason for trying to get out of jury duty.

When it was my turn to talk to the clerk, I proudly explained that we were expecting our fourth child, which was due at any moment. I expected the clerk to coo with delight and maybe wish me mazel tov. Instead, she berated me in front of everyone in the office.

The angry clerk asked in a loud voice, "How can you have four children when the world is overpopulated? You're a drain on the planet!"

I put up with her lengthy lecture in silence—and was rewarded with that exemption. As I walked away, I overheard the next woman in line explaining her jury-duty excuse: she was a contestant on *The Biggest Loser* and couldn't miss her only chance for reality television fame and fortune. Not only did she get her exemption, but the clerk insisted on having her picture taken with the future celebrity. If that doesn't illustrate our society's shift in priorities, I don't know what does.

In our environmentally conscious age, anyone who wants to be considered enlightened has to demonstrate concern for endangered species. So we hear a lot about the plight of the panda and the polar bear. We hear a lot less about the real endangered species: humanity.

In every apartment we've lived in, my children have been outnumbered by the other tenants' dogs. When the new 24/7 organic market opened up across from us, I noticed that the dog food section was right next to the baby food section—and that the dog food section was a lot bigger.

What about Overpopulation?

In some circles these days, having a large family is considered a crime against humanity. My offspring are a plague on the planet, and I'm a carrier. The idea that having children is bad for the environment isn't as new as many people think and in fact turns out to be greatly exaggerated.

Back in the 1970s, overpopulation was the global warming of its day. The average man or woman wasn't really sure how or why, but experts told them the planet couldn't support more people, and that was good enough for them. It was the subject of a *Time* magazine's cover story, so it had to be true. In one episode of *All in the Family*, Archie Bunker's daughter and her hippie husband, "Meathead," explained their (short-lived) decision to remain childless with the then-fashionable alibi that it would be a crime to bring another child into this horrible world.

But as a chorus of demographers have pointed out, those experts' doomsday predictions didn't come true. Not only is there enough food to sustain the world's population, but food prices are declining while distribution has improved exponentially. Economist Amartya Sen won a Nobel Prize for proving that famines aren't caused by natural droughts but by all-too-human political corruption.[1] Another Nobelist, Simon Smith Kuznets, demonstrated that "more population means more creators and producers, both of goods along established production patterns and of new knowledge and inventions."[2]

That theory, in turn, explains why—contrary to claims about our over reliance on fossil fuels—"in the America of 1850, you needed an average of 4.6 tons of petroleum equivalent to produce $1,000 of goods and services. By 1950, you needed only 1.8 tons, and, by 1978, 1.5 tons."[3] After 1978, this figure dropped to 0.8 ton[4] and is forecast to decline an average of 2.9 percent each year to 2015.[5]

Economists in the past warned that we were running out of coal, oil, and other raw materials, yet inevitably, a new source of these fuels was discovered somewhere on Earth. Every generation has witnessed human innovators developing new ways to harvest resources and use them more efficiently and cheaply.

What about Our Carbon Footprint?

"Having children is the surest way to send your carbon footprint soaring," declared Kate Galbraith in the *New York Times* at her *Green* blog in 2009. "Take, for example, a hypothetical American woman who switches to a more fuel-efficient car, drives less, recycles, installs more efficient light bulbs, and replaces her refrigerator and windows with energy-saving models," Galbraith wrote. "If she had two children, [Oregon State University] researchers found, her carbon legacy would eventually rise to nearly 40 times what she had saved by those actions." [6]

Around the same time, the United Kingdom's Optimum Population Trust (OPT) launched a "Stop at Two" online pledge, imploring couples to limit their family's size for environmental reasons. "Having more than two children is irresponsible," declared OPT's Jonathan Porritt, who also runs the British government's Sustainable Development Commission. "Every additional human being is increasing the burden on this planet which is becoming increasingly intolerable." [7]

For individuals who are even more environmentally conscious, the preferred slogan seems to be "Two Is Too Many." They're using environmentalism as their trendy, socially acceptable excuse not to have any children at all.

"Meet the women who won't have babies — because they're

not eco-friendly," trumpeted the *Daily Mail* in a widely remarked upon profile of women skipping motherhood altogether for the sake of Mother Earth. "Having children is selfish. It's all about maintaining your genetic line at the expense of the planet," said thirty-five-year-old environmental activist Toni Vernelli, who put her convictions into practice by getting sterilized at age twenty-seven.[8]

Her motivations don't sound entirely selfless to me: "Ed and I married in September 2002, and have a much nicer lifestyle as a result of not having children. We love walking and hiking, and we often go away for weekends. Every year, we also take a nice holiday—we've just come back from South Africa." Conveniently enough, Toni and Ed have calculated that they're allowed to have "one long haul flight a year."[9]

At least she's practicing what she preaches. Some of the people scolding the rest of us to reduce our carbon footprint can't claim with a straight face to be doing so themselves.

"We're going to have to live with less," movie director and million-dollar eco-donor James Cameron told the *Los Angeles Times*. The *Times* left out the "inconvenient truth" that Cameron owns three homes (none of which have solar panels) totaling twenty-four thousand square feet—or ten times the size of the average American house. He also has a helicopter, three motorcycles, and a fleet of vehicles that includes "a Humvee fire truck," whatever that is.[10]

Ironically, speaking of overpopulation, Cameron has four children. So does Al Gore. Ted Turner—whose apocalyptic rant opened this chapter—advocates a Chinese-style one-child policy for America, but he has five children of his own.

Prince Charles warned delegates to the 2009 Copenhagen climate change conference "there were now only seven years left to save the planet." Oddly enough, the prince's personal annual carbon footprint is more than 2,500 tons—including the 6.4 tons he emitted just to fly to that conference. Meanwhile, the average British citizen's carbon footprint is only 11 tons.[11]

In terms of hypocrisy, it's hard to top the Voluntary Human Extinction Movement. Around since the early 1990s, the Voluntary Human Extinction Movement tells followers, "When every human chooses to stop breeding, Earth's biosphere will be allowed to return to its former glory."[12]

Which invites the question: so why can the rest of us still hear you talking?

If we stopped having children tomorrow, the rest of us would continue to live—longer than ever before, in fact. The aging have carbon footprints, too. Is the next step a campaign of "involuntary human extinction" of the elderly for the sake of the planet? And if so, exactly who will supervise this dystopian *Logan's Run* program?

As for my fellow Brooklynites with their Jack Russell terriers and cocker spaniels: don't animals have carbon footprints, too?

Little Cities in the Big City

In fact, families with children don't place the burden on the environment that critics say they do, especially in urban areas like the one I live in. Urbanization is being hailed by many as the wave of the future. Big cities are no longer the polluted centers of waste and disease they once were when they were villainized in the early days of the Industrial Revolution. Due to population density, public transportation, and municipal green energy initiatives, many American cities have smaller carbon footprints than some rural areas.

The same logic applies to families compared to single adults living alone. Think about it: my family of four children doesn't have six separate tubes of toothpaste going at once. My family is a little city in the big city.

Driving my wife and kids in one vehicle uses up no more gas than a single person tooling around in the same car. We vacation together, eat together, shop together, and so on.

Families learn to conserve their limited resources. The biggest family on reality television, the Duggars, is criticized for what detractors imagine is the size of their nineteen-child carbon footprint. However, as the family patriarch explained in one episode, the Duggars embrace stewardship of the Earth, and as a result, they buy (and sell — it's the family business) only used cars, as well as used appliances, and they live debt free. Hand-me-down clothing and simple toys are a way of life. So is buying in bulk. It would be hard to imagine a family farther removed from our wasteful consumerist culture.[13]

My children and I are learning how to care for Planet Earth by reading *Curious George* together as our families favorite fictional monkey learns to "reduce, reuse and recycle." I hope to send them out into the world with a healthy regard for the environment as well as other human beings. It seems to me that many well-meaning eco-warriors care about the environment only, not the people in it, and that doesn't seem very balanced to me.

Education rather than annihilation is the answer. If we teach children about healing our planet and conserving resources, they will do that when they're grown up, too.

Words of Wisdom

Jewish tradition tells us that children and the environment are not mutually exclusive. "Be fruitful and multiply" also promotes respect for nature and embraces conservation, animal welfare, species preservation, sanitation, and pollution reduction. The Talmud covers prohibitions against atmospheric, water, and even noise pollution,[14] and Deuteronomy even tackles issues of waste disposal.[15]

When God created the first couple, he sent them out to "fill the world and conquer it."[16] Today we think of conquest as exploitation. However, that wasn't part of those instructions.

The Midrash elaborates. When God created the first man, he took him around to all the trees in the Garden of Eden and said to him, "See my handiwork, how beautiful and choice they are . . . Be careful not to ruin and destroy my world, for if you do ruin it, there is no one to repair it after you."[17]

Thus, children and the environment are not mutually exclusive. Having children and caring about the environment don't cancel each other out. In fact, they go hand in hand.

PART 3

The Third Trimester:

Why Parenthood Makes Sense

Chapter 7

SPIRITUAL LEGACY:
The Real Secret to Life after Death

A grandchild is God's reward for raising a child.
—Bill Cosby

$\mathcal{D}$AVID WAS THE first of my crowd of old high school friends to lose a parent. When his father died a few years back, it brought home to all of us that our own mothers and fathers wouldn't be around forever, either.

David told me that he was inconsolable until right after the funeral, when his wife uttered two little words that changed everything: "I'm pregnant."

Nine months later, David named his first son after his late father. This is a Jewish custom that serves to keep the person's name and memory alive and forms a metaphysical connection to the past. We also hope the child will be inspired by the good characteristics of the late relative.

This simple gesture symbolizes a traditional concept we don't hear much about anymore (except when heads of state worry — often too late — about how they'll be remembered): the idea of leaving behind a legacy.

Legacies versus Lifestyles

A legacy is something — a name, a reputation, an achievement — that we hand down to our descendants. As people have fewer children — or none at all — the notion of leaving a human, flesh-and-blood legacy sounds quaint.

In the twenty-first century, we value today rather than yesterday and tomorrow. We embrace instant gratification. The phrase "saving up to buy something" is as old-fashioned as dial-up Internet. Just a few generations ago, Americans had more money in their savings accounts than they owed in debt; today, the numbers are reversed.[1]

As the world demographically flips upside down, so have our lifestyle choices. Consider the increased use of pets as surrogate children. It's become commonplace for female celebrities (and women who aspire to be like them) to take their toy dogs everywhere they go, often dressed in small costumes and carried in designer bags.

Trends like this, no matter how odd, aren't limited to millionaire celebrities for long. In 2010, Americans were reportedly spending more money on their pets than on their children.[2]

Pets can be loyal, beloved companions and are even believed to help their owners' physical and mental health. Pets love us unconditionally (well, dogs do, anyway), whereas children are prone to yell "I hate you!" after all we've done for them. (On the other hand, kids eventually do learn to take care of their own poop.) However, the fact is that caring for a dog (or a cat) and caring for a child are two very different matters.

I wonder if one reason pets have become so popular is the morbid fact that animals don't live longer than their owners. The idea used to be that our (human) children would care for us in our old age and maybe take over the family business. When a child died before a parent, we noted sadly that such a tragedy was outside the natural order of things.

One generation overlapped another, traditions were handed down, and those who died lived on in the memories (and the genes) of their offspring. In other words, everyone left a legacy.

This idea is illustrated in the following Talmudic story:

An old man was planting a tree. A young person passed by and asked, "What are you planting?"

"A carob tree," the old man replied.

"Silly fool," said the youth. "Don't you know that it takes seventy years for a carob tree to bear fruit?"

"That's okay," said the old man. "Just as others planted for me, I plant for future generations."

The Joys of Grandchildren

Another case for kids is that you get to experience the joys of having grandchildren — or at least you get a shot at having them. That's not something we think about until it is too late.

As the old joke goes, "If I'd known having grandchildren was this much fun, I'd have had them sooner!"

King Solomon, who was called "the wisest of all men" for a reason, used the analogy of a threefold cord: "Though one may be overpowered, two can defend themselves. A cord of three strands is not quickly broken."[3] He reminds us that a one-strand cord is weak by itself, a two-strand cord is stronger, and a three-strand rope is stronger than either. When children have children of their own that creates a threefold cord.

Your children will bring you and your parents closer in ways that years of therapy never can. Having children of my own allowed me for the first time to have an honest adult relationship with my parents. We had newfound respect for each other as we realized we had suddenly become peers. For the first time in my life, I sought out my parents' advice (and boy, did I need it).

Even other people's grandchildren can bring joy to seniors. Once a month, I visit our local nursing home and host a Sabbath party for the residents. I enjoy doing it, and they seem to like my songs and jokes, even if they have heard them many times.

What these seniors love even more than my jokes are my children. When I bring them along to the party, the residents go crazy over them. I can almost see the long-ago child awakened in each of them.

Just as married men statistically live longer than unmarried men, grandparents live longer than seniors without grandchildren. Maybe grandchildren give seniors something to look forward to. Maybe they re-energize their grandparents when they visit or even call. Never underestimate the importance of basic human contact to our physical and psychological health.

How Will We Be Remembered?

When we die, no one will remember our petty business dealings or the grade we got on a long-forgotten exam. All our earthly accomplishments will suddenly retreat into the background, and those we leave behind will remember only *bubby's* (grandma's) chicken soup or the candies *zady* (grandpa) used to keep in his pockets just for the kids.

In death, our social standing no longer matters. To illustrate this, Jewish law mandates that every person, no matter how great and powerful, should be buried in a modest wooden casket without metal handles or even nails. Such a casket will disintegrate in the ground, allowing the body to return to the earth as quickly as possible, thus enabling the soul to attain true and final peace. In fact, if a coffin is not mandatory by local law, burial without a coffin is the most preferable option. The Torah reminds us, "Unto dust shall you return."[4]

The message is clear: the deceased can't appreciate an ornate casket, and those who might be impressed by such a display have their priorities upside down. In the end, all of us will be judged not by our sports car or golf average or fancy coffin, but by our good deeds. We will live on in the memories of the family we leave behind.

The Grandchildren Shortage

When my wife's grandmother — an eighty-five-year-old Holocaust survivor — plays with her two-year-old great-granddaughter, that unique personal interaction is something no video game or chat room can simulate. It is true interactivity and — in the end — the only one that matters.

Unfortunately, as men and women put off having children, their own parents are becoming grandparents much later in life. In turn, grandchildren have less time to grow close to their grandparents and learn from them.

In America, grandparents aren't an endangered species quite yet. But believe it or not, that isn't the case in Europe. [5] And if present sub-replacement fertility birthrates abroad continue, the result will be a new type of family unit—one that does not include any siblings, cousins, uncles, or aunts.

The only biological relatives for a lot of people will be their ancestors. In other words, there will be "family trees without branches." [6]

An Extraordinary Legacy

"If you leave a child or grandchild, you live forever." So said New York resident Yitta Schwartz shortly before she died at age ninety-three. That was the reason she gave her family when she discouraged them from keeping photographs of her. When the *New York Times* decided to devote considerable space to her obituary, the family was therefore reluctant to provide a photograph to the paper. [7]

Why did the most famous newspaper in the world want to commemorate this unknown woman? Because her life had been so quietly extraordinary. "She left behind 15 children, more than 200 grandchildren and so many great- and great-great-grandchildren that, by her family's count, she could claim perhaps 2,000 living descendants." Having survived the Holocaust and immigrated to America, Yitta was believed to have "generated one of the largest clans of any survivor of the Holocaust—a thumb in the eye of the Nazis."[8]

Like many Hasidim, Mrs. Schwartz considered bearing children her tribute to God. A son-in-law, Rabbi Menashe Mayer, a lushly bearded scholar, said she took literally the scriptural command that "You should not forget what you saw and heard at Mount Sinai and tell it to your grandchildren."[9]

Words of Wisdom

One of the most beautiful concepts the Hebrew Bible gave the world was the notion of God as a parent, not just a power. We are enjoined to call him our Father. As God said through the prophet Isaiah, "Like one whom his mother comforts, so will I comfort you."[10] Becoming mothers and fathers and leaving a legacy provides us with a unique opportunity to model God's selfless parenthood.

God chose Abraham to be the founder of a new faith not because of his great military prowess or his wealth or his gifts as a public speaker. God declares, "I have chosen him so that he will teach his children and his household after him to keep the way of the Lord, doing what is right and just."[11]

What made Abraham and Sarah special in God's eyes was simply that they embraced the responsibilities of parenthood. Sarah and Abraham had children very late in life. In fact, Sarah laughed off the idea that she could conceive at her advanced age. Yet faced with God's plan for her, she eventually welcomed the awesome and unexpected opportunity to do God's will without knowing how this miraculous unexpected situation would work out. Abraham and Sarah had no retirement plan or day-care arrangements or line of credit. Yet they stepped out in faith and were rewarded beyond measure.

God's relationship with Sarah and Abraham was holy. Our relationships with our pets or even our friends or colleagues simply do not have this incomparable status. Ultimately, only the parent-child relationship approximates the sacred.

"Honor your mother and father, that your days may be long, in the land which the Lord your God gives you."[12] That's the only one of the Ten Commandments that reveals the reward we get for following it. We can interpret that to mean that not only will we live a long life, but that life will be blessed and fulfilling. If we have children who honor us, that promise is passed along to them and then to their descendants. Now that's a legacy.

Chapter 8

YOU DON'T HAVE TO HAVE KIDS
TO LEARN FROM THEM
(But It Helps)

Sarge: *We done our duty. Andy's grown up.*
Soldier One: *Let's face it—when the trash bags come out,*
                  we army guys are the first to go.
                — *Toy Story 3*

I DON'T USUALLY CRY at movies, but when I went to see *Toy Story 3*, I was glad I had those ugly 3-D glasses to hide behind. In this surprisingly moving finale to the *Toy Story* trilogy, we learn that the toys' beloved Andy is no longer a little boy. He's now seventeen years old and has moved on to bigger, less cuddly toys like video games and electric guitars.

Andy's also about to start college. While packing to leave, he has to decide what to do with his old friends like Buzz Lightyear and Woody the Cowboy. Unfortunately, the toys he fully intends to store in the attic to hand down to his children one day end up at the Sunnyside Daycare Center instead — where they are horribly mistreated. Luckily, the toys escape and are briefly reunited with Andy before he leaves them behind with a little girl who promises to care for them.

I know I wasn't the only grownup who shed a tear watching *Toy Story 3*, maybe because the poignant theme of lost innocence is such a universal one, with Andy's toys representing that childlike purity we all once possessed.

Note the anachronistic fact that Andy's favorite toys, like Mr. Potato Head, are plastic relics from the 1960s — those long-ago days when children like the *Toy Story* filmmakers were being born. *Toy Story 3* shows Andy "putting away childish things" when he becomes (more or less) an adult. In reality, today's dorm rooms and frat houses are packed with toys, such as collectible dolls (I mean, action figures) still in their boxes.

Today's twenty-something "kids" buy toys for themselves instead of for the children they don't have yet and maybe never will. While I've spent this whole book making the case for having children, I realize that no matter what I say, some men and women won't ever have children, either by choice or due to circumstances beyond their control.

What Children Can Teach Us

I still believe all these people can learn a lot from children. I know I have.

As I wrote this, New York City was blitzed with snow. Once again, I was marooned at home with the kids.

Kids love snow because it's wet, it's messy, and there's no school. Parents hate snow because it's wet, it's messy, and there's no school. I decided to put my stranded status to good use and ponder all the lessons I've learned from my children. More accurately, I *tried* to ponder, but the kids were making too much noise.

Here's what I managed to come up with. These are just some of the ways we can all learn from children, even if we don't have children ourselves.

Homework Stinks! Have Fun Instead!

My middle son, Eli, attended a Montessori school where the children don't have homework and are encouraged to be creative and curious. I really envy him. As kids, we'd dream of the day when we'd never have to do homework again, but how many of us still take a different kind of work home every night? My investment banker friends consider it a short day if they get home before midnight. Sure, they can order in from a great restaurant and have lots of other perks, but is that really how they imagined their life would be? Do they have a lot of laughs?

Children laugh at the dumbest things and for the longest time. (Just ask a kid to tell you a "knock knock" joke.) They seem to instinctively know that laughter is healthy for our minds and bodies.

Smiling is serious business. Children rate their activities based on how much fun they're having. Can you add a little more fun to your workday to recapture that spirit?

Children also live in the moment. We may joke about their short attention span, but that characteristic has its advantages. For example, it keeps them from holding grudges for years like adults do.

In addition, children laugh about four hundred times a day on average. Adults laugh only about fifteen times. We can learn a lot from children about being happy.[1]

Nothing in Life Is Free

There's a reason eight-year-olds don't have credit cards, although I'm sure the banks would love it. I've tried to instill in all my children the old-fashioned notion of saving up your money to buy a new toy. This disciplined idea was hard enough to get across to children and some adults back when our grandparents lived that way. Everything in our contemporary culture contradicts that ancient financial wisdom, so I have to battle all the messages my children get from the media and the other adults in their lives.

I also teach my children to give. Giving is a habit that has to be developed early in the home. It's one of the foundations of our faith. My children take great delight in giving to charities. That, too, contradicts many of the messages they're bombarded with.

As the chair of religious affairs at Pratt Institute, I like to give my children an idea of what I do all day (and sometimes all night), to convey to them the importance of having a vocation, especially one that involves helping others. When I tell them I can't play with them all day because I have to work (except during snowstorms!) they understand, in their own small way, because I've taken them on tours of our campus.

On one of those tours, my elder son, Mendel, asked me, "Where do the students learn?" I pointed to the beautiful workshops. When he asked, "Where do the students eat?" I pointed to the well-appointed cafeteria. When he asked, "Where do the students sleep?" I pointed to the campus dormitory.

Finally, he asked the best question of all: "Daddy, who pays for all of this?"

I was proud of him for figuring out so early that nothing in life is free.

Ask Questions

Children ask lots of questions, like "Why is the sky blue?" It's a habit that drives many adults crazy, but kids do indeed love to ask questions. Not only that, they need to. Their growing minds are thirsty for knowledge.

Most of us quickly forget what that yearning feels like, yet without it, we wouldn't be who we are today. Some fortunate adults never lose that natural, insatiable curiosity. Those men and women are the world's innovators and artists. It's telling that many geniuses make their greatest discoveries and creations when they are still fairly young.

Adults often deny their natural curiosity. They're afraid to ask "stupid" questions—or maybe to learn something they'd rather not know. One of the bravest acts is giving ourselves permission to be curious once more.

Use Your Imagination

My daughter, Orah, is happier playing with the cardboard box than the toy that came in it. That's not uncommon. In fact, it's such a universal phenomenon that in 2005, the cardboard box was officially inducted into the National Toy Hall of Fame.

My baby, Yaakov, doesn't even need a box. With a mother, father, and three siblings in the house, he likes to just sit in his chair, suck on a pacifier, and take in all the action. He reminds me that sometimes it's good to sit back and just watch the circus around us.

Our kids pick up on everything we do, including our careers, which they try to understand in their own inimitable way. Having watched me scribbling at my desk day in and day out, each of my kids has set up his or her own little office space in the living room. I can never find my office supplies anymore because the kids keep "borrowing" them to put in their own desk drawers. I was annoyed about this until their mischief helped me realize I sometimes take my work too seriously. Aren't so many of us just overgrown kids, still "playing office" at our jobs?

Be Open to Children

While I believe that having children is both an obligation and a privilege, it's not a privilege we all experience. For those who are not childless by choice and who have tried without success to have sons and daughters of their own, this situation can be a painful one. From the rude, thoughtless questions from well-meaning (and sometimes not-so-well-meaning) relatives and strangers to the expense and discomfort of fertility treatments that aren't guaranteed to work, many childless couples feel misunderstood, frustrated, and hopeless.

Those who don't have children may feel wracked with guilt or a sense of personal failure. Some may blame religion for instilling this guilt, but it is a myth that "barren women" are cursed by God.

In the stirring words of the prophet Isaiah: "Let not the barren one say, 'Behold, I am a dry tree.' For so says the Lord to the barren ones who will keep My Sabbaths and will choose what I desire and hold fast to My covenant: 'I will give them in My house and in My walls a place and a name, better than sons and daughters; an everlasting name I will give them, which will not be discontinued." [2]

Even if we don't have children, by being open and welcoming to the children we encounter in our lives, we won't just learn a new way of looking at the world. We'll be truly blessed.

Ironically, one of the most famous childless women in the world is known for her dedication to helping children.

Thinking back to her own journey from her disadvantaged childhood to the heights of wealth and fame, Oprah Winfrey said about the child-centered charities she has founded, "I realized in those moments why I was born, why I am not married and do not have children of my own. These are my children. I made a decision to be a voice for those children, to empower them, to help educate them, so the spirit that burns alive inside each of them does not die."[3]

Only a few men and women in any generation will attain Oprah Winfrey's riches and influence. However, all of us can "beget" children—whether spiritually or physically—if we are willing to do so. Think about mentoring, teaching, volunteering, and coaching. Not only do you make a memorable impact on the children you help, but they help you too.

In the Talmud, Judah Hanasi wrote, "I learned much from my teachers, more from my colleagues, and most from my students."[4] Mentors teach, but they also learn. As someone responsible for guiding a child on the right path, you will have to stay on that path yourself. Mentoring often forces us to raise our own standards of behavior because we are now setting an example for others.

Words of Wisdom

You may be surprised to find out that according to Jewish tradition, even those who have no biological children of their own can still "give birth" in other ways.

The Bible notes, "These are the offspring of Aaron and Moses on the day God spoke with Moses at Mount Sinai,"[5] and then lists the names of the sons of Aaron—but not those of Moses. Why?

In the Talmud, the sages tell us that although Aaron is indeed the father of his sons, Moses *taught* Aaron's sons.[6] They are, in a sense, Moses' spiritual children. Therefore, there was no need to mention Moses' name. His influence on them was understood.

In this same section of the Talmud, the sages offer examples of children who have "parents" other than just their biological mother and father. In this way, teaching and caring for children other than one's own is singled out for special honor.

A powerful example of this lesson is my spiritual mentor: Rabbi Menachem Schneerson. He was better known as the Lubavitcher Rebbe and affectionately called "the Rebbe" by his many followers.

World leaders sought his sagely advice, and his schedule was exhausting. Yet the Rebbe always made time to greet children with special warmth and affection. He also established the world's largest Jewish children's organization, Tzivos Hashem.

Sadly, the Rebbe and his wife of sixty years never became parents. Yet upon his passing, he left thousands of orphans around the world, each one of whom had been nurtured by his powerful spiritual message and his personal example of unconditional love.

Chapter 9

POSTMODERN PARENTING:
The New Radical Counterculture

*Even one kid running around my villa makes me nervous,
so I'm definitely not a candidate for father of the year!*
— George Clooney

$\mathcal{W}$HEN P. D. James' novel *The Children of Men* came out in
1992, it was categorized as science fiction. Like all great vision-
ary writers, James sensed danger looming and tried to warn the
rest of us. Today, with a worldwide demographic crisis reach-
ing critical mass, her dystopian fiction reads more like fact.
Perhaps one day, *The Children of Men* will be re-catalogued
in the Dewey decimal system as nonfiction—assuming any
of us survive that long.

Set in 2021, the novel presents a world in which the human race can no longer reproduce. The last generation, called the "Omega" children, was born in 1995. James cunningly describes what such a planet would be like. For one thing, the silence is deafening. For another, the only thing that grows and thrives is decay: "The children's playgrounds in our parks have been dismantled. For the first 12 years after Omega the swings were looped up and secured, the slides and climbing frames left unpainted. Now they have finally gone and the asphalt playgrounds have been grassed over or sown with flowers like small mass graves. The toys have been burnt, except for the dolls, which have become for some half-demented women a substitute for children."[1]

I sometimes get the eerie feeling that I'm living in a prequel to *The Children of Men*. As a rabbi at a big city college, I often walk around the campus with my brood. Students and faculty alike always run over and start smiling and cooing when they see my children. My kids are cute—but they aren't *that* cute. It's almost as if these young adults and (ironically) their teachers have never seen actual children before. Sadly, some of them probably haven't, at least not for a while.

In *The Children of Men*, men and women stop reproducing because they no longer can. All the world's men suddenly and mysteriously become infertile. In our world, the birthrate is dropping throughout the Western world because so many men and women no longer *want* to reproduce. Choice by choice, they're bringing James' fictional nightmare scenario to life. Stranger still, they seem to want it that way. If an evolutionary biologist observed this kind of behavior in any other species, he (or more likely, she) would conclude the species was willingly committing suicide!

Who Will Show Up for the Future?

I've noticed that the students I see every day are getting older and older all the time and staying in school longer than students of their parents' generation. They tell themselves—and we tell our children—that they need to go to college to get a good job so they can achieve a high standard of living, presumably to support a family one day.

But the "family one day" part seems more and more like an afterthought, if not something they studiously avoid. We've joked for decades about "Animal House" and "party colleges" and observed that university has become a four-year (or longer) holiday from responsibility. Yet the jokes no longer seem as funny. As we've seen throughout this book—and simply by looking around us—more and more young people, especially young men, are stretching their extended adolescence through their twenties and into their thirties. They're going from adolescence to a kind of obsolescence.

Few of them pause to consider what their life choices will mean for the future. I don't mean just their personal future (one in which they've morphed into the single, fat, lonely, and unlovable Comic Book Guy from *The Simpsons*) but the future of the world.

If that sounds melodramatic, hear me out. Pretend you're P. D. James for a moment. Try to imagine a near future, say, fifty years from now. The mayor of New York is a Hasidic Jew. The president of the United States is a Mormon. Europe is under radical-Muslim control, and Sharia law is enforced. Sorry, would-be backpackers: those marijuana cafés and red-light districts were torched years earlier.[2]

In other words, people of faith are in charge. If that sounds either implausible or like a satirical report Jon Stewart might deliver with rolling eyes on *The Daily Show*, consider the hard facts and statistics from demographer Phillip Longman: "What's the difference between Seattle and Salt Lake City? There are many differences, of course, but here's one you might not know. In Seattle, there are nearly 45 percent more dogs than children. In Salt Lake City, there are nearly 19 percent more kids than dogs."[3]

In his book *Shall the Religious Inherit the Earth?*, Eric Kaufman states that people of faith are more likely to have children, regardless of income. Kaufman believes that this religious fertility will eventually overturn the secularization process that has been underway in the West since the 1960s.[4]

I'm a religious person (that's an understatement!), but I'm also a campus rabbi who treasures diversity. The world that's coming isn't exactly diverse. Let's put it this way: *The Daily Show*, or anything like it, probably isn't going to be a big hit.

What's Next?

The world has entered uncharted history. All those "happy, advanced" (and almost childfree) European countries—the same ones Americans are often scolded to emulate—have too few children to replace their existing populace. Their expensive utopian lifestyles will give way to social unrest. We saw this for ourselves in the summer of 2011, as riots broke out from England to Israel. I saw the same shops I used to frequent in my hometown of Manchester burned to the ground by young people burdened by decadence or debt.

In the fall of 2011, the tensions experienced across Europe landed on American shores. The Occupy Wall Street movement began in New York City and spread across the rest of the country, with chanting protesters camping out in tents by the hundreds to express their disillusionment with the economic order.

We're learning to our dismay that progress doesn't always go in one direction. From Greece to Great Britain, a post-parenting future looks bleak. As for the United States, we have trillions of dollars in unfunded entitlement obligations such as Social Security, Medicaid, and Medicare. No money is left in the trust funds that were originally set up to pay for these programs. The money was borrowed decades ago for still more government programs and paid back in IOUs.

The answer to these problems doesn't necessarily lie in outsourcing, either. Immigrants and newcomers to these countries may not share their new nation's values and within a couple of generations, their own birthrates tend to decline.[5]

Meanwhile, China's official one-child policy is reaping what it has sown: millions upon millions of young men with no hope of ever finding a bride. Into what will they channel all that excess energy and primal frustration? War? With us, perhaps? What have they got to lose? And who will we send to fight them? Will we even bother?

Why "Childfree" People Might Make the Best Parents

The purpose of this book has not been to preach and proselytize. Well, maybe a little. It's part of my job description. I don't think the childfree movement is mad, just misplaced. I respect the decisions these people make, even if I disagree with them, as long as they are made carefully and compassionately.

However, when I began this book, I did see the childfree movement as selfish. Now I realize I was being naive and simplistic. In fact, in many cases, childless couples choose to be so for what they consider altruistic ideals. The irony is that the reason they give for not wanting kids is the reason they would make the best parents: they care about the future of our planet.

For all their thoughtfulness, they haven't quite thought through the implications of their decision. Quite simply, without children, there will be no future to either save or destroy.

An example of a thoughtful person who is a non-parent is actor George Clooney. At age fifty, he has a "no kids policy." He has said, "I'm so selfish and I get nervous around kids, and I know I'm not ready for that kind of life. I've settled into a very comfortable lifestyle and I really don't want to change things."[6]

It's odd that Clooney, whose philanthropy is almost as famous as his acting career, would call himself "selfish." With his generosity and commitment to causes he believes in, I can't help but think about what a great father he would probably be.

A few years ago, Clooney played a character with the same "no kids" philosophy. In Up in the Air, he portrayed Ryan Bingham, who is the opposite of a corporate headhunter: Bingham doesn't hire people on behalf of other companies; he fires them.

Bingham's job obliges him to fly across the country virtually nonstop, something most people would find grueling but he savors. Not surprisingly, his phrase to describe other people (who make unreasonable demands on his time and attention) is "excess baggage." His biggest goal in life is to acquire enough frequent flier points to make it into an airline's exclusive "ten-million-mile club."

However, a series of surprising events convince him he's missing out on a normal life. Bingham screws up the courage to seek out his favorite "no questions asked" girlfriend and tell her about his decision to settle down and raise a family—with her. Unfortunately, one of those questions they never asked each other was, "Are you married?" As Bingham finds out when he turns up unexpectedly on her doorstep, she already is—and has no desire to leave her husband and children and run off with him.

Dejected, then enlightened, Bingham hands over a large chunk of his precious ten million air miles to his newlywed sister to pay for the honeymoon she couldn't otherwise afford. In helping her start a family, Bingham reveals a newfound openness to the idea of domesticity. We're left thinking he's on his way to someday starting one of his own.

Will the real life George Clooney ever experience a similar epiphany? For his sake, I hope he does.

Clooney did in fact become a parent, if only on the big screen, in his next major movie, *The Descendants*. In that award-winning film, he played Matt King, a self-proclaimed "back up parent" who suddenly has to take his role more seriously when a boating accident puts his wife into an irreversible coma. His once distant relationship with his two daughters changes overnight and he is forced to face everything he has avoided or been blind to for years, such as his wife's affair with a local real estate agent. It isn't easy, but over the course of the film, King's relationship with his daughters gets stronger, as he's forced to grow up and accept his responsibilities.

Give Kids a Chance

In all cultures around the globe, increased television watching leads to a decrease in birthrates. A University of Michigan study notes that in Brazil, where television was introduced province by province, a direct correlation exists between the amount of time a Brazilian woman watches domestically made *telenovelas* and how many children she will have. These programs, like the soap operas produced throughout most of Western culture, depict a world where children are a boring financial drain.[7]

It's true kids can be annoying—very annoying (my apologies to my children, who might read this someday). On a recent Sabbath, as I tried to take an afternoon nap, I was awakened by screams. One of my darling boys had stuck a plastic arrow into another delightful son's eye. Instead of napping, I spent my afternoon in the emergency room. As tired as I was, I was elated to learn that his eye was going to be fine. (All I had to do was keep the whole incident secret from his *bubby*.)

For a brief moment that Saturday, the thought of life without one of my children flashed before my eyes. It was worse than the most staggering nightmare.

So maybe I'm trying to do the impossible: persuade you to give kids a chance, even though the real joys of parenthood can only be experienced, not explained.

Words of Wisdom

While I have tried to focus on all the intellectual reasons for having children, along with some spiritual ones, I must mention one argument that goes beyond reason. Logic and reason absolutely have their place, but there's a lot to be said about intuition, too.

In Yiddish, we have the word *nachas*. It's untranslatable, but "the joy, blessings and pride we get from our children and grandchildren" will have to do. So we might say, "May your new child give you much *nachas* in years to come."

And as every mother and father knows, sharing our *nachas* with anyone who will listen is one of the best parts of being a parent. *Nachas* needs to be experienced to be understood.

So let's end with a story from my firstborn.

At 5:30 one morning, my son Mendel woke me up with some earth-shattering news. (I just realized this book makes it sound like I sleep a lot! Believe me, I don't get much chance. When you have kids, sleep becomes a very serious matter.)

"Daddy," Mendel loudly declared, "I have been thinking about something, and I have come to a decision! I would no longer like you to buy me Play Mobil! From now on I would only like you to buy me Lego!"

"Mendel! It's 5:30 in the morning. Guess what? I'm buying you nothing."

Then after a few minutes of (guilty) pondering, I found myself moved by my son's accidental profundity. Having spent hours on my hands and knees playing with my children, I knew the difference between the two popular toys.

Playmobil toys are beautiful and intricate but also lifeless and static. The most work you have to do with Playmobil is to open the box.

But when you open a Lego box, that's when the work—which is really more like play—begins. You draw a plan, put the bricks on top of each other, tear them down, redo your plan, and then rebuild. Lego involves creativity and artistry. Lego is like life.

So I went into Mendel's room and told him that, yes, I'd start buying him Lego instead.

As I write this, Mendel's new baby brother is just a few months old. I'm tired, thanks to so many sleepless nights and 3:00 a.m. feedings plus trying to arrange car pooling and daily commutes. What matters is that his siblings are so happy to have him. They don't even care that he isn't made of Lego bricks.

My children are the most enriching, rewarding, and beautiful part of my life. They are also the most draining and stressful. After writing this book, I could just as easily write another one making the case against kids. I get that. Logically, kids are expensive, time consuming, and physically, emotionally, and psychologically draining, but as I have tried to show, they are also so much more.

It's time to stop playing and start building.

EPILOGUE

It's 10,000 times better than anything I've ever done.
—Steve Jobs on fatherhood

*E*ACH YEAR DURING the New York Marathon, my children and I watch the runners come down Bedford Avenue in Brooklyn. (And every year, I pledge that next year I will run the marathon. And every year, I don't.)

When you're sitting in a more-or-less comfortable chair on the sidelines, running looks easy. Yet we all know it isn't.

To run the marathon, you'd need to train and prepare. In fact, to finish fairly respectably, you'd probably have to alter your whole way of daily living and endure a lot of pain and inconvenience. Yet imagine the rush when you cross that finish line!

Parenthood is the greatest experience the world has to offer. Please don't turn it down just because it seems too difficult. When you finally hold your newborn baby in your arms, as I have, you may wonder why you ever waited so long.

DISCUSSION QUESTIONS

1. The author writes: "Throughout the Western world, young men and women are doing everything in their prime reproductive years except reproducing." Why are an increasing number of people postponing marriage and parenthood? What are the advantages and disadvantages of this decision?

2. Do the rewards of parenthood outweigh the sacrifices one must make to be a parent? Has the book influenced your opinion about this? If so, how?

3. The author asserts that, due to an increase in the economic opportunities for many women today, the "opportunity cost" of motherhood has dramatically risen. Is this a sufficient reason to put off parenthood? What are the advantages and disadvantages of this decision?

4. The author points out that that the global population is aging and that the increase in population is not caused by a population boom but rather by medical advancements keeping older people alive longer. Do you agree or disagree? If you agree, what are the implications of this assertion?

5. The author points out that couples are labeled "selfish" for choosing a large family. How many children do you consider the ideal family size? Are children in larger families are more neglected than children in smaller ones?

6. The author is critical of the increased use of social networking, citing the rise of "Friend" as a verb instead of a noun in the era of Facebook. Is a virtual online family just as good, if not better, than a real one? Does social networking foster the dangerous illusion that we're connected and engaged with each other, when we really aren't?

7. Is the lack of money a valid reason to postpone parenting? Should you wait until you can give your children the best material things in life before becoming a parent? Has this trend has been encouraged by the media, and if so, how?

8. The author includes studies showing that having children makes one less happy. Do you think parenthood will bring you happiness? How do you define happiness?

9. Are children bad for the environment? If so, should government legislate population growth, to help decrease the global carbon footprint?

10. Have you ever thought about the notion of "leaving a legacy?" If so, what legacy would you like to leave and how would you like to be remembered after you are gone?

11. Even if you don't want to have children, do you think there is a benefit from interacting with children? What lessons would you like to impart on children and what lessons do you think children can impart on you?

12. The author highlights the growing birth rates in faith-based communities, which defy the downward trend in so many other segments of the population. Why do you think that this particular group is having larger families?

Is there a downside if one particular faith demographic grows larger than others?

13. The author asserts that, "In many cases, couples choose to be childless for what they consider altruistic reasons. The irony is that the reason they give for not wanting children is the reason they would make the best parents." In other words, thoughtful individuals who care about society's future would be the very best parents of all. Do you agree or disagree?

NOTES

Introduction

1. Lauren Sandler, "The Only Child: Debunking the Myths," *Time*, July 8, 2010.
2. Mary Elizabeth Williams, "Is Motherhood Natalie Portman's 'Greatest Role'? Salon.com, February 28, 2011, http://www.salon.com/2011/02/28/natalie_portman_most_important_role/.
3. Charles A. Donovan, "Bend the Baby Curve Like Beckham," Oregon-Live.com, August 2, 2011, http://www.oregonlive.com/opinion/index.ssf/2011/08/bend_the_baby_curve_like_beckh.html.
4. Michael Kimmel, *Guyland: The Perilous World Where Boys Become Men* (New York: Harper Collins, 2008), 4.
5. A. Scott Berg, *Kate Remembered* (New York: Putnam, 2003), 55.

Chapter 1

1. Kay S. Hymowitz, "The New Girl Order," FrontPageMag.com, October 15, 2010, http://www.manhattan-institute.org/html/miarticle.htm?id=3316.
2. Kate Bolick, "All the Single Ladies," *Atlantic*, November 2011, http://www.theatlantic.com/magazine/archive/2011/11/all-the-single-ladies/8654/.
3. Hanna Rosin, "The End of Men," *Atlantic*, July/August 2010. http://www.theatlantic.com/magazine/archive/2010/07/the-end-of-men/8135/#].
4. Allan C. Carlson, "'Anti-Dowry'? The Effects of Student Loan Debt on Marriage and Childbearing," *The Family in America* 19, no. 2, (December 2005), http://www.profam.org/pub/fia/fia_1912.htm.

5. Maureen Dowd, "Blue Is the New Black," *New York Times,* September 19, 2009. http://www.nytimes.com/2009/09/20/opinion/20dowd.html.

6. Lisa Belkin, "Do Gen X Women Choose Work Over Kids?" *New York Times,* June 30, 2011, http://parenting.blogs.nytimes.com/2011/06/30/gen-x-women-choose-work-over-kids/.

7. Tina Fey, "Confessions of a Juggler: What's the Rudest Question You Can Ask a Mother?" *New Yorker,* February 14, 2011, http://www.newyorker.com/reporting/2011/02/14/110214fa_fact_fey.

8. Ibid.

9. Bolick, "All the Single Ladies."

10. Frank W. Baker, "Media Use Statistics," Media Literacy Clearinghouse, http://www.frankwbaker.com/mediause.htm.

11. US Census Bureau, "Estimated Median Age at First Marriage, by Sex: 1890 to the Present," November 2011, http://www.census.gov/population/socdemo/hh-fam/ms2.xls.

12. Ryan Kelty, Meredith Kleykamp, and David R. Segal, "The Military and the Transition to Adulthood," *Transition to Adulthood* 20, no 1 (Spring 2010), http://futureofchildren.org/publications/journals/article/index.xml?journalid=72&articleid=526&sectionid=3616.

13. Num 32:4.

Chapter 2

1. Paul R. Ehrlich, *The Population Bomb* (Cutchogue, NY: Buccaneer Books, 1995), 6.

2. Phillip Longman, "The World Will Be More Crowded—with Old People," *Foreign Policy,* September/October 2011, http://www.foeignpolicy.com/articles/2011/08/15/the_world_will_be_more_crowded_with_old_people.

3. Nicholas Eberstadt, "The Demographic Future: What Population Growth—and Decline—Means for the Global Economy," *Foreign Affairs* 89, no. 6, November/December 2010, 55.

4. Ibid.
5. United Nations Population Division, Department of Economic and Social Affairs, *World Population Prospects: The 2010 Revision* (New York: United Nations, 2011), http://esa.un.org/unpd/wpp/index.htm.
6. "Falling Fertility," *Economist*, October 29, 2009, http://www.economist.com/node/14744915.
7. Russell Shorto, "No Babies?" *New York Times*, June 29, 2008, http://www.nytimes.com/2008/06/29/magazine/29Birth-t.html?pagewanted=all.
8. Justin Gillis and Celia Dugger, "U.N. Forecasts 10.1 Billion People by Century's End," *New York Times*, May 3, 2011.
9. Eberstadt, "The Demographic Future, 55.
10. Ibid., 58-59.
11. Gen. 1:28.

Chapter 3

1. Xavier Lur, "If Facebook Were a Country, It Would Be the Third Most Populated," *Tech Xav*, March 19, 2010, http://www.techxav.com/2010/03/19/if-facebook-were-a-country/.
2. Ben Quinn, "Social Network Users Have Twice as Many Friends Online as in Real Life," *Guardian*, May 8, 2011, http://www.guardian.co.uk/media/2011/may/09/social-network-users-friends-online.
3. Andrea Bartz, Matt Bigelow, Eric Kroh, and Anna Maltby, "Coffee Houses, Still Growing Fast, Want the Bigger Bucks in Supermarkets," Medill Reports-Chicago, December 5, 2007, http://news.medill.northwestern.edu/chicago/news.aspx?id=72415.
4. David Zax, "Alone Together: An MIT Professor's New Book Urges Us to Unplug," *Fast Company*, January 13, 2011, http://www.fastcompany.com/1716844/alone-together-an-mit-professors-new-book-urges-us-to-unplug.
5. Gen. 24:67.

6. Lee A. Lillard and Constantijn Panis, "Health, Marriage, and Longer Life for Men" (Santa Monica, CA: Rand Corporation, 1998), http://www.rand.org/pubs/research_briefs/RB5018.

Chapter 4

1. US Department of Agriculture, Center for Nutrition Policy and Promotion, "Expenditure on Children by Families, 2009, "Miscellaneous Publication No. 1528-2009, http://www.cnpp.usda.gov/publications/crc/crc2009.Pdf
2. Phillip Longman, *The Empty Cradle: How Falling Birthrates Threaten World Prosperity and What to Do about It* (New York: Basic Books, 2004), 75.
3. Dave Ramsey, "Budget Implications of Having a Baby—These Little Blessings Don't Have to Break the Bank!" Daveramsey.com, February 9, 2010, http://www.daveramsey.com/article/budget-implications-of-having-a-baby/lifeandmoney_budgeting/.
4. Pamela Paul, "How Much Does a Baby Really Cost?" *Redbook*, n.d., http://www.redbookmag.com/money-career/tips-advice/money-baby-cost-4.
5. Julia Scheeres, "A Satellite Baby-Sitting Service," *Wired*, May 2, 2002, http://www.wired.com/science/discoveries/news/2002/05/52253.
6. Judith Warner, *Perfect Madness: Motherhood in the Age of Anxiety* (New York: Riverhead Books, 2006), 16.
7. Mark Steyn, *After America* (Washington, DC: Regnery Publishing, 2011), 287.
8. http://techcrunch.com/2012/07/16/marissa-mayer-the-first-ever-pregnant-ceo-of-a-fortune-500-tech-company/
9. Babylonian Talmud, Kiddushin 31a.
10. Ibid.

Chapter 5

1. Jennifer Senior, "All Joy and No Fun: Why Parents Hate Parenting," *New York Magazine,* July 4, 2010, http://nymag.com/news/features/67024/.

2. Martin Regg Cohn, "How to Measure Gross National Happiness," Thestar.com, September 15, 2009, http://www.thestar.com/comment/article/695624.
3. Senior, "All Joy and No Fun,"
4. Ibid.
5. David McRaney, "Procrastination," *You Are Not So Smart* (blog), October 27, 2010, http://youarenotsosmart.com/2010/10/27/procrastination/.
6. Lenore Skenazy, *Free-Range Kids: How to Raise Safe, Self-Reliant Children (Without Going Nuts with Worry)* (San Francisco: Jossey-Bass, 2010).
7. Ps. 126:5.

Chapter 6

1. Colby Cosh, "Random Browsing Day," Colbycosh.com, August 18, 2004, http://www.colbycosh.com/old/august04.html.
2. Jonathan V. Last, "The Problem with Shrinkage," *Weekly Standard*, December 13, 2006, http://www.weeklystandard.com/Content/Public/Articles/000/000/013/012mveoc.asp.
3. Jonathan V. Last, "The Good and Bad of a Population Drop," *San Diego Union-Tribune*, November 29, 2006, http://www.signonsandiego.com/uniontrib/20061129/news_lz1e29last.html.
4. Heather L. Ross, "Producing Oil or Reducing Oil: Which Is Better for U.S. Energy Security?" *Resources* 148 (Summer 2002).
5. "Energy Intensity Declines but Global Economy Hit by Rising Oil," Commodity Online, April 15, 2011, http://www.commodityonline.com/news/Energy-intensity-declines-but-global-economy-hit-by-rising-Oil-38177-3-1.html.
6. Kate Galbraith, "Having Children Brings High Carbon Impact," *Green* (blog), August 8, 2009, http://green.blogs.nytimes.com/2009/08/07/having-children-brings-high-carbon-impact/.
7. Margaret Ryan, "Is It Selfish to Have More Than Two Children?" BBC News, February 18, 2009, http://news.bbc.co.uk/2/hi/uk_news/magazine/7884138.stm.

8. Nastasha Courtenay-Smith and Morag Turner, "Meet the Women Who Won't Have Babies Because They're Not Eco Friendly," *Daily Mail,* November 21, 2007. http://www.dailymail.co.uk/femail/article-495495/Meet-women-wont-babies—theyre-eco-friendly.html.

9. Ibid.

10. Guy Adams, "James Cameron Labelled Climate Change 'Hypocrite,'" *Independent,* October 24, 2010, http://www.independent.co.uk/environment/climate-change/james-cameron-labelled-climate-change-hypocrite-2115151.html.

11. Mark Steyn, "Climate Hypocrites, " *National Review,* December 9, 2009, http://www.nationalreview.com/articles/228835/climate-hypocrites/mark-steyn.

12. The Voluntary Human Extinction Movement, "About the Movement," http://www.vhemt.org/aboutvhemt.htm.

13. Lori Kerrigan, "The Duggars: How Many Is Too Many?" Parenting Squad, February 10, 2010, http://parentingsquad.com/the-duggars-how-many-is-too-many

14. Babylonian Talmud, Baba Batra 2.

15. Deut. 23:12.

16. Gen. 1:28.

17. Midrash, Eccles. Rabbah 7:13.

Chapter 7

1. Michael Snyder, "10 Charts That Embody Everything That's Wrong with the U.S. Economy," Business Insider, February 16, 2011, http://www.businessinsider.com/charts-debt-unemployment—2011-2#household-debt-has-soared-to-almost-unbelievable-levels-over-the-last-30-years-4.

2. Pete Wedderburn, "American Parents Now Spend More Cash on Pets Than They Do on Their Children," *Telegraph,* December 13, 2010, http://blogs.telegraph.co.uk/news/peterwedderburn/100067886/american-parents-now-spend-more-cash-on-pets-than-they-do-on-their-children/.

3. Eccles. 4:12.
4. Gen. 3:19.
5. John Mauldin, "Global Aging and the Crisis of the 2020's," *Business Insider,* January 12, 2011, http://www.businessinsider.com/global-aging-and-the-crisis-of-the-2020s-2011-1.
6. Mark Steyn, "Quartet of Ladies Shows Where We're Headed," *Jewish World Review,* November 27, 2006, http://www.jewishworldreview.com/1106/steyn112706.php3.
7. Joseph Berger, "God Said Multiply, and Did She Ever," *New York Times,* February 19, 2010, http://www.nytimes.com/2010/02/21/nyregion/21yitta.html.
8. Ibid.
9. Ibid.
10. Isa. 66:13.
11. Gen. 18:19
12. Exodus 20:12.

Chapter 8

1. Sharon Biggs, "Many Children Laugh a Lot Every Day Even If No One Is Telling a Joke," Examiner.com, September 20, 2009, http://www.examiner.com/parenting-education-in-newark/many-children-laugh-a-lot-every-day-even-if-no-one-is-telling-a-joke.
2. Isa. 56:3-5.
3. Jeanne M. Nagle, *Oprah Winfrey: Profile of a Media Mogul* (New York: Rosen Publishing Group, 2007), 127-128.
4. Babylonian Talmud, Ta'anit 7a.
5. Lev. 3:1.
6. Babylonian Talmud, Sanhedrin 19b.

Chapter 9

1. P. D. James, *The Children of Men* (New York: Grand Central Publishing, 2002), 12.
2. Stanley Kurtz, "Europe's Religious Future?" *National Review,*

October 18, 2006, http://www.nationalreview.com/corner/130416/europes-religious-future/stanley-kurtz.

3. Phillip Longman, "The Liberal Baby Bust," *USA Today*, March 13, 2006, http://www.usatoday.com/news/opinion/editorials/2006-03-13-babybust_x.htm.

4. Eric P. Kaufman, *Shall the Religious Inherit the Earth? Religiosity, Fertility and Politics*, n.d., http://www.sneps.net/research-interests/religious-demography.

5. Fjordman, "What Does Muslim Immigration Cost Europe?" *Global Politician*, May 10, 2007, http://www.globalpolitician.com/22773-euroimmigration.

6. "George Clooney's No Kids Policy," AskMen.com, May 2, 2007, http://www.askmen.com/celebs/entertainment-news/george-clooney/george-clooney-no-kids-policy.html.

7. W. Bradford Wilcox and Carlos Cavallé, "The Sustainable Demographic Dividend: What Do Marriage and Fertility Have to Do with the Economy?" Social Trends Institute, October 3, 2011, http://sustaindemographicdividend.org/articles/the-sustainable-demographic.

INDEX

ABOUT THE AUTHOR

SIMCHA WEINSTEIN is an internationally known speaker and the best-selling author of Up, Up, and Oy Vey: How Jewish History, Culture, and Values Shaped the Comic Book Superhero and Shtick Shift: Jewish Humor in the 21st Century. He has appeared on CNN and NPR and has been profiled in leading publications, including the New York Times, Miami Herald, and London's The Guardian. A syndicated columnist, he writes for the Jerusalem Post, JTA (Jewish Telegraphic Agency), the Royal Shakespeare Company, Condé Nast, and many other agencies. He chairs the Religious Affairs Committee at Pratt Institute, the renowned New York art school. He was recently voted "New York's Hippest Rabbi" by PBS affiliate Channel 13.

Visit Simcha Weinstein
at *www.rabbisimcha.com*

Follow him on Twitter @RabbiSimcha